dare
to
dream

Stories

of 16 people

who became

somebody

dare to dream

Stories

of 16 people

who became

somebody

• • •

WILLIAM **O'MALLEY,** S.J.

ave maria press AmP notre dame, indiana

© 2009 by Ave Maria Press, Inc.

Founded in 1865, Ave Maria Press is a ministry of the Indiana Province of Holy Cross.

www.avemariapress.com

ISBN-10 1-59471-201-8   ISBN-13 978-1-59471-201-2

Cover image © jiunlimited.com.

Cover and text design by John R. Carson.

Printed and bound in the United States of America.

To
John Costello, S.J., and John Poduin

Contents

• • • • • • • • •

Introduction

• • • • • • • • • • • • • •

Since you were old enough to sit up in your Pampers on the family-room couch, the tube has been selling you self-centeredness every waking hour of the day. Not a single student I've taught in the last forty years doubts that accumulating enough money, fame, sex, and power is the course to greatness. But if that were true, how do you explain Elvis Presley, Marilyn Monroe, Janis Joplin, Jimi Hendrix, Jim Morrison, John Belushi, River Phoenix, Kurt Cobain, and the others who "had it all"? Did they anesthetize themselves with drugs for years and finally kill themselves because they were so *happy*? Yet every kid I've taught believes those people were *successes*. Now that really is grade–A+ brainwashing!

Societies all over the earth, in song and story, have publicized the deeds and lives of men and women who have acted *better* than most ordinary folks—more resilient, nobler, readier to rise to daunting challenges: Odysseus, Abraham, Judith, Gilgamesh, Psyche, Socrates, Jesus, El Cid, King Arthur, Joan of Arc, and uncountable others. Nowadays, however, in dramatic contrast, our society trumpets the deeds and lives of people who are *worse* than most of us would want to be—athletes who cheat, entertainers who numb themselves with drugs, entrepreneurs who readily betray their peers. Can anyone explain how people who do those things came to become noteworthy?

What this book is asking you to ponder, for yourself, is the lives of people who have lived by far different norms

1

than amassing money, fame, sex, or power. None of them is or was a flawless saint, but each seems to have lived a life more substantial than merely accumulating objects and publicity. They seem to have lives more intensely *human* than gyrating chimpanzees in a media circus or plastic princesses on the covers of *People* and *Star* magazines.

Humans Are Not Animals!

What separates us from other animals is that we can learn, love, and grow more intensely human by more learning, loving, and growing. Or not.

Let's say that we dare to dream. How do these skills serve us?

Learning. Any stag can "know" a hunter is chasing him, but the animal doesn't say to himself, "What the heck did I do to *that* guy?" Human beings have at least the *potential* to ask "why," the central question. We have the capacity to *understand*, which no other animal we know has. Objective fact: Human beings are the only species that suffers from conscience.

Loving. Animals show affection for their own, to the point of sacrificing their lives for them, but humans can sacrifice their lives—often without dying—for people they don't even *like*. Ask any teacher about that! Genuine love is not just a feeling. It's an act of the will, a commitment that takes over when the feelings fail, when the beloved is no longer even *likable*. Ask any parent!

Growing. No lion can become more leonine, but human beings can become more intensely human. It's inarguable: Abraham Lincoln was a better (more moral) human being than Adolf Hitler. How do we know that? By the way they both acted, by the choices they made, by the way they treated other human beings, by the order of their priorities.

Consider the following pairs:

Marble: Acorn = Cub: Baby

At a quick glance, those pairs look more or less similar. The marble and acorn are about the same size and shape; the cub and the baby act more or less the same. But they're profoundly different. Plant the marble and acorn, and the marble's just going to lie there; it hasn't the potential to be anything other than what it is. But the acorn has at least the *potential* to become something enormously larger than what it is: a huge oak tree. Or not. It could fall onto a sidewalk and wither or into a swamp and rot, but it does have the capability of changing into a size and shape unrecognizably different. In the same way, both the cub and baby will both grow physically, but the cub is never going to be any more bear-like than it was from the start, while the human baby has the *potential* to become Thomas Jefferson or Helen Keller. Or not.

Therefore, humanity is a spectrum, ranging from pimps, pushers, and terrorists at one end (human, but just over the line from beasts) all the way to great-souled human beings like Christopher Nolan and Oprah Winfrey, two heroes featured in this book. The intention of these stories is to lure you further along that spectrum of humanity than you originally planned—and certainly further than the media are urging you to go.

Picture a blanket with babies of all races crawling around it, fascinated by one another's differences, endlessly curious and full of wonder. Now picture the usual subway car or bus: dead-ended faces staring into oblivion, slumped shoulders, and suspicious glances. What got lost? The basic purpose of these stories is that you can discover what that potential is (for yourself) and resolve that you, for one, are by God *not* going to lose it.

Objective Morality Does Not Change

Life is filled with objective facts. For example, human beings have a different genetic makeup from bunnies or carrots or rocks! Subjective opinions do, in fact, differ from age to age, from society to society, from individual to individual, *but* subjective opinions are valid *only* when they're backed up by objective evidence. For a long time people believed the earth was flat. They were wrong. How do we dare say they were wrong? Objective facts.

This book's foundation is the objective fact that each of us is a human and not merely a rational animal (just an ape with an implanted computer). Human beings have more inner value than bunnies or carrots or rocks. Related to this truth is that we live in a web of moral (human) relationships with every other inhabitant of this fragile planet. That is the human invitation. Education has been referred to as the *humanities* because it is intended to encourage us to become more fully human. The purpose of education has always been to train good citizens, men and women of character. Read these stories and the virtues of character they represent with the intention of becoming a good spouse, a good parent, a good person. Achieve that, and the rest of your goals (e.g., attending a good college, becoming an attractive job candidate) will take care of themselves.

Character Is Your Genuine Self

Everyone has a personality; not everybody has character. An old adage taught that you should date someone with a lot of personality but that you should marry someone with a lot of character.

Personality is a set of habits of coping that we develop, without thinking or judgment, before we're three years old. It is our personality that allows us to react instinctively to our unique parents, siblings, and environment. Some infants try to satisfy (even anticipate) unspoken demands and become introverted. Others resent such intrusions, rebel, and become extroverted. Neither type of personality is better than the other; each has assets and liabilities, and since they were formed before a child could think, neither type is blameworthy. The crucial realization is that either personality type is not an incurable inherited disease. Shy people can develop confidence, and aggressive people can develop thoughtfulness and empathy—as many of the true stories in these pages will demonstrate.

On the other hand, *character is the true self you are when no one is watching.* Character is a person's own, individually reasoned and accepted *principles* about how a decent human being would act in given situations—and how he or she would not act. Character is not just a matter of knowing *that* such an act is approved or disapproved in this particular society—or even that it is objectively degrading to other human beings and to oneself. Character means *interiorizing* that truth, feeling it, caring about it. Character is not just a realization but a *conviction.* Most of the time, even in moral debates, we know what the right thing to do is. The tough part is having the conviction that we *ought* to do it, even if it costs us something.

Character also equates with personal conscience. Evolving a personal conscience depends on *both* of the powers of the human mind: reason (critical thinking) and intuition (it "makes sense").

A good way of asking the basic question is, Where does the "ought" come from in "I ought to . . ."? For instance, parents *ought* to feed their infants and keep them warm. Why? Because of the objective facts, because of what the infant is and what the parent is in relation to him or her. In the same way, we ought to be grateful to our parents, at the very least for the gift of life. We ought to show respect for every human being. We ought to be kind, responsible, honest, persevering. Why? The objective fact is that each of us is an equally human being. It would be inescapably wasteful to ignore or refuse our shared invitation to be human together.

The French sociologist Emile Durkheim wrote, "To teach morality is neither to preach nor to indoctrinate. It is to explain." The stories in this book help us to examine values accepted by all cultures in history as essential for being fulfilled human beings. These stories help us to answer, What does the objective nature of humanity demand of each of us?

Moral questions are inevitable. We live in a world where all the other porcupines have quills, too, and different agendas. You can't become a good person, a good spouse, a good parent until you've wrestled with what makes someone a good (moral) human being. You can't study literature without evaluating moral (human) choices. Studying morality is a matter of survival as human beings.

What will make us humanly fulfilled, happy, more alive than merely "getting by"?

Come and see.

How to Read the Stories

• •

There are stories of sixteen people in this book. These people really did (and do) live in the same world that we do! A common quality of each person is that they started out life as a "nobody." The success and fulfillment they each achieved came about only through the course of climbing over or through a great many unpleasant obstacles.

Each story begins with a word and definition that expresses a virtue lived by that person. Also, a famous quotation and a Scripture passage that embodies that virtue is a further way for you to help connect the person's story with your own experience.

The stories are meant to encourage you and inspire you to make more of your life. Several "Points to Ponder" are included with each story. Use these for your own personal reflection. You may even want to use them to start a conversation with your peers or some adults. They can also be the basis for journal entries.

General Questions for Every Chapter

A wise man named Aristotle once said that you learn courage by *acting* courageous, even if you are convinced you're not. How are these words true of anyone learning to be richly human? This and other general questions can be applied to each story. Besides the "Points to Ponder" specific to every story, take some time to ponder these basic questions as you read about the everyday heroes in this book:

- How did the person connect with the virtue listed at the beginning of the story?
- How did that person really embody and give undeniable testimony to that virtue?
- What were the factors *inside* that person that simply wouldn't allow him or her to settle for being a blotch on the wallpaper?
- What people helped the person in the story overcome fear to reach for something more than just survival? In what specific, concrete ways did those people help the person's life come super alive?
- What were the obstacles for this person?
- What were the inner resources the person had to call on? How did the person learn he or she had these inner resources?
- How does this person's story affect you?
- How does this person's story make you think you could make a difference in the world? Specifically, how does it inspire you to make a difference in your family, at school, at work?

Finally, think for a minute or two as you complete each story. Ask yourself: "If I could meet this person, what would I want to ask him or her?" Quite likely, it wouldn't be: "What is the color of your nail polish? What is your GPA? How much can you lift?" Would it?

one

····

Christopher Nolan

Poet

1965–2009

Confidence:

Pronunciation: \kän-fə-dən(t)s\
Function: *noun*
Date: 14th century
1 a: a feeling or consciousness of one's powers or of
reliance on one's circumstances **b:** faith or belief that
one will act in a right, proper, or effective way

◇◇◇

Work like you don't need the money,
Love like you've never been hurt,
And dance like no one is watching.

—Anonymous

◇◇◇

*For God did not give us a spirit of cowardice but rather of power
and love and self-control.*

—2 Timothy 1:7

I t might seem odd—even brash—to write an autobiog-
raphy at twenty-two. But Christopher (Christy) Nolan
had ample justification. At only fifteen, he had won
two writing prizes and published a book of poems that
respected critics compared to William Butler Yeats, James
Joyce, and Dylan Thomas—despite the fact he'd been
crippled with cerebral palsy since birth. As he describes
it, "his drunken, drooling body," his "spoiled manhood,
birth-brain damaged" often lashed uncontrollably and
poked an unwary bystander in the face or gut—or worse.
He couldn't chew or speak more than a yowl or control
his bowels or bladder. "The frenzied limbs could wreak
involuntary havoc yet he was unable to brush a fly from
his nose." (Christy could nod his head, pound the foot
of his wheelchair with his feet, signal his needs with his
eyes. And he could weep. And he could laugh. Yet all the
while he drank in the world inexhaustibly with his ears
and eyes, "fiercely listening, nestled in hassled lucidity,"
wrapping what he knew in webs of words no one would
unwrap until he was eleven.

He had almost died at birth. His tiny body was in
a transverse position across the birth canal, his spine
wedged into a V-shape by his mother's contractions, cutting off oxygen from his brain for two hours before he was
delivered by cesarean section. Any new infant completely
changes his family's whole schedule and priorities for
a year or two, but Christy's homecoming changed their

lives forever. Here was a child who would never be toilet-trained, never be able to feed himself, and never learn to get up when he fell. Yet his parents refused to buckle. Their twisty boy was going to be as loved and challenged as any other boy. "His mother it was who treated him as normal, tumbled to his intelligence, tumbled to his eye-signaled talk." He drew strength from Bernadette Nolan's courage, and humor from her down-to-earth, no-nonsense love: "Come on, Christopher, don't be so damn dramatic." Trusting her faith in him, he slowly found "home," that is, confidence. "She spoke resurrecting hope when there was no hope at all."

When Christy was seventeen months old, his mother took him to a Dublin doctor who was intrigued by the inquisitive baby, studying *him* back! He played games with the child, blowing in his eyes so Christy shut them; then the doctor stopped, and the boy popped his eyes open to see what was wrong. The doctor knew what Christy's mother knew. He suggested physiotherapy, speech therapy, occupational therapy, and, in time, schooling at the Central Remedial Clinic in Dublin.

When he was four, Christy's mother took him to a psychologist, who assured her that his intellect was superior, equivalent to a seven- or eight-year-old's. But still he couldn't speak. Except with his eyes.

Christy's father worked a one-day-on, one-day-off schedule as a psychiatric nurse so he could also tend his farm in Corcloon, fifty-five miles west of Dublin. There the boy grew, nestled like any normal boy between his father's knees as he drove the tractor, wheeled from place to place in a wheelbarrow before he was big enough for a wheelchair, which "allowed him access to birds' nests, anthills, and sheep farts." His father took him to football matches, but most importantly he sat his wobbly boy on his knee and recited poetry to him and told him nursery rhymes and all sorts of bawdy stories. He "meddled in medleys of cheery but breathtakingly beautiful thought. Words seemed his tools of trade as he ferreted for mollification in his bondaged world."

His sister might be (because of her age) the most remarkable member of a truly extraordinary family. "She cradled his head when he was sick but when he was well she gave him hell." One day when they were older and he involuntarily grabbed her bosom, she merely sniffed, "Let go, you sex maniac." When she was seven and he was five, their parents gave her a speckled Connemara pony as a birthday gift. When Christy signaled with his eyes that he wanted a try, at first she refused, but he sat "determined to look hurt and bruised," and finally she said, "Look here, brat, I'll give you one ride, that's all." With one parent on each side, they heaved him tottering into the saddle and followed beside him, he demanding to go faster. They even allowed him a jump. As his mother said, "Falling off is less painful than not having a chance."

During the same year, the family uprooted itself from the farm to move to Clontarf, three miles north of Dublin, to be near the Central Remedial Clinic. It was a school filled with all kinds of children with disabilities from slight to more severe. There Christy encountered superbly sensitive teachers who earned his trust and vice versa. "The mute boy became constantly amazed at the almost telepathic degree of certainty with which they read his facial expressions, eye movements, and body language. . . . It glimmered in their kindness to him. It glowed in their keenness, it hinted in their caring, indeed it caressed in their gaze."

At age eleven, Christy was set free at last, by a typing teacher named Eva Fitzpatrick and by a new drug, Lioresal, which calmed his spasms—somewhat. With Eva soothing his panicky nerves, cupping his chin, and with a stick banded to his forehead ("the unicorn stick"), Christy began giving wing to his imprisoned soul, one letter at a time. "But for Eva Fitzpatrick, he would never have broken free." And after a while, "his belief now came from himself." One day, when Eva pretended to be called away, she asked Christy's mother to support his head for a moment. His mother could *feel* the need in his head, pulling her hands to the right letters.

Finally, it became time for Christy to move to a secondary school. His father told a psychiatrist friend his son's applications kept being refused, and Christy brashly conversed with the two in his own language, "leaving no doubt in the doctor's mind that here was a boy ready and willing to face school life bravely, if only a school would have him." The doctor got on the phone, and within minutes the boy was scheduled for an interview at the Mount Temple School. Despite Christy's terror and sweats, John Medlycott, the headmaster, looked at this glaring, drooling, punching, gibbering boy and said, "Well, Joseph, when can you start?"

The principal enlisted two understandably skittish boys to wheel Christy from class to class, wipe his drooling face, and over the months begin to intuit his mute signals. "He was full of hope for he sensed the sincerity and kindness in them." Gradually, three or four more boys and girls joined them until finally he became their taken-for-granted brother: "Lift up your feckin' head until we see what you're saying." They became his lifeline to the world of school, and much later Christy would be the inspiration for the song, "Miracle Drug," written by one of his Mount Temple classmates named Paul David Hewson, now known as Bono.

"My mind is just like a spin dryer at full speed; my thoughts fly around my skull, while millions of beautiful words cascade down into my lap. Try then to imagine how frustrating it is to give expression to that avalanche in efforts of one great nod after another." But nod he did, a single page taking a whole day's work of tapping out letters. Then he cajoled his mother to send his boyhood story to the Spastics Society Literary Contest in London. To everyone's astonishment, he won first prize. On Christmas Eve, he heard eminent Britons interviewed on BBC about the most important moment of their year, and Edna Healey, an author, wife of the Chancellor of the Exchequer, said the high spot of her year had been reading Christy Nolan.

When he had won the prize again the following year, the London *Sunday Times* wrote an article about him, soliciting funds to buy Christy a computer. Thousands of pounds poured in, enough to inaugurate a drive to highlight the communication needs of "tongue-tied but normal-rational man," and to fund research for new mechanisms to open and free their minds and souls.

Then, when he was only in his third year of secondary school, Christy's book of poems, *Dam-Burst of Dreams*, was published, and within ten days it was on the best-seller list. The BBC did a documentary on Christy and his family, and from all over Europe came reporters from radio, magazines, and newspapers. Only one, an American, showed less than profound respect for the boy. He sat unsmiling, wrote nothing, yawned as Christy showed him how he typed. When the magazine finally appeared, the article was a shock. The American had written that the entire Christy Nolan phenomenon was a total fraud; a boy of fifteen—much less a wreck of a child—couldn't possibly have written the boyhood story or the poems; it was obviously his mother's work, using a freak to get notoriety. That night, Christy cried "tears of pristine despair."

In 1987, Christy Nolan's autobiographical novel received the $35,000 Whitbread Award. His mother read his acceptance speech: "Tonight is the happiest night of my life. By choosing my book as the Book of the Year, you have fashioned me as an equal to any other writer, be they creating words by hand or by head."

Christy had his dark moments. Yet he was indomitable, just as his parents and sister were. When someone asked if he ever felt despair, he typed his response: "No. I haven't time."

Points to Ponder

1. Try to list all the taken-for-granted things and people you rely on to give you a secure sense of confidence. Imagine the effect on your life if they were all suddenly ripped away, as in a hurricane or a fire. What would that be like?

2. Can you remember a time when someone—seemingly without any real basis—made you feel they "understood" you, had a gut instinct you had more to you than even you suspected? What concrete, specific ways did they show this feeling? Why do you suspect they even noticed you at all? How do you think you are sensitive to other people that same way?

3. Have you ever felt drawn to a particular well-written phrase or sentence? If such occasions are infrequent (or non-existent), what could be the reason? Do you think it could be the degrading language of commercials, music lyrics, or iPod chatter? What kept Christy from being "tone deaf" to language? What relation does that sensitivity have to the sensitivity to others mentioned in point two above?

two

• • • •

Oprah Winfrey

• • • • • • • • • • • • • • • •

Television Host, Media Mogul, Philanthropist

1954–

Gratitude:

Pronunciation: \gra-tə-tüd\
Function: *noun*
Etymology: Middle English, from Anglo-French or
Medieval Latin; Anglo-French, from Medieval Latin
gratitudo, from Latin *gratus* grateful
Date: 1523
1. Thankfulness; consciousness of a benefit received

◇◇◇

The test of all happiness is gratitude; and I felt grate-
ful, though I hardly knew to whom. Children are grateful
when Santa Claus puts in their stockings gifts of toys or
sweets. Could I not be grateful to Santa Claus when he
put in my stockings the gift of two miraculous legs?
—Gilbert Keith Chesterton

◇◇◇

*Consider this: whoever sows sparingly will also reap sparingly,
and whoever sows bountifully will also reap bountifully. Each
must do as already determined, without sadness or compulsion,
for God loves a cheerful giver.*

—2 Corinthians 9:6–7

On November 12, 1991, a black woman sat before
the all-male, all-white Judiciary Committee of
the United States Senate to testify on behalf of a
bill she herself had written with the assistance of Illinois
Governor James Thompson and Senator Joseph Biden of
Delaware. She had been moved to this unprecedented act
by the rape and murder of a four-year-old Chicago girl,
Angela Mena, by a man twice convicted of child molesta-
tion and twice released early from prison. She wanted a
national data bank of offenders convicted of child abuse
that would be made available to schools, scouting troops,
and other child-centered organizations. And she got what
she came for. President Bill Clinton signed the bill into law
in 1993.

Why did she bother? At the time, Oprah Winfrey
was the second-highest money-making personality in
the world. Every day, 16 million people watched her
talk show on television. She had been nominated for an
Academy Award, won Emmys, and also received the *Ms.
Magazine* award for Woman of the Year. She had interviewed politicians and celebrities far more "important"
than little Angela Mena. Why did she bother? One reason
was that she herself had been a victim of sexual abuse
as a child. When she was nine, she had been raped by a
nineteen-year-old cousin. Until she was fourteen, she was

repeatedly raped by her mother's boyfriend and an uncle. And she wasn't going to take it any more. "My mission," she said at the time of the bill, "is to use this position, power, and money to create opportunities for other people." She felt gifted and grateful for her good fortunes, and that helped to impel her to give gifts in return.

Oprah Winfrey was born January 29, 1954, in the tiny town of Kosciusko, Mississippi. She spoke later of her conception as resulting from "a one-day fling under an oak tree." Her father, Vernon, lived 250 miles away and was unaware Oprah's mother, Vernita Lee, was even pregnant until he got a birth announcement along with a scribbled message: "Send clothes." Vernita had intended to name the child Orpah after the sister-in-law of the biblical heroine Ruth, but the midwife was not a great speller, so the girl became Oprah and began what was not to be a very easy young life.

In her earliest years, she lived with her grandparents on their tiny pig farm, while her mother was off someplace trying to find work. "The nearest neighbor was a blind man down the road. No playmates, no toys except for one corncob doll. I never had a store-bought dress. It was very lonely out there." Her grandmother was a tough old lady who nonetheless made Oprah feel, without words, that she was cherished. Her grandmother also forced her to learn how to read and write long before she ever went to school.

The one haven in her childhood before she went to school was the Baptist church, where she was asked to read from the Scripture and to act in pageants with other children. Her first pageant performance was when she was only three; she practiced her lines by reciting them to the pigs and chickens. The adults found her charming, but the other kids definitely did not, sneering, "Here come Miss Jesus" at her.

At home her grandparents expected complete and literal obedience, often sending her out for a tree branch to whip her with. Her grandfather terrified her. "You couldn't even cry! You got whipped till you had welts on your back. Unbelievable. I used to get them every day because I was precocious." And yet she also said, "I am what I am because of my grandmother. My strength. My sense of reasoning. Everything." When Oprah finally attended kindergarten, she was bored silly with the childish games and wrote a letter to her teacher about it. Surprisingly, the teacher understood her position and promoted her into first grade and very soon after into third grade.

When Oprah was seven, she became too much for her aging grandmother to handle, so Oprah was sent off to Vernita, who by then earned her living cleaning houses in Milwaukee for about $50 a week, plus welfare payments. Mississippi had been hard, but Milwaukee was heartless, and Vernita was at her wit's end trying to provide for Oprah and for another daughter. So within a year, she arranged for Oprah to go to her father, Vernon, and his wife, Zelma, in Nashville. Vernon was a hard worker, moving up from scrubbing pots to become a maintenance person at Vanderbilt University. "Zelma was real tough," Oprah said of her stepmother, "a very strong disciplinarian, and I owe a lot to her because it was like military school there." And the little girl continued to give her recitals—in churches, for women's groups, and at banquets. One of her favorite performances was to recite William Ernest Henley's poem "Invictus," which could well describe her own life:

> Out of the night that covers me,
> Black as the Pit from pole to pole,
> I thank whatever gods may be,
> For my unconquerable soul.

But just as she was beginning to feel at home in Nashville, at the age of nine, she received word that Vernita had finally married the father of her third child and wanted her back in Milwaukee for the summer. Oprah went to Milwaukee, expecting to return to her father in time for school. But when Vernon came for her in August, Vernita refused to let her leave, and since she and Vernon had never married, he had no legal rights in the matter. Oprah was painfully unhappy. Her mother was always working or "out," so Oprah spent her time reading or numbing herself with TV. But while she was at the Lincoln Middle School, a teacher named Gene Abrams noticed that Oprah was always alone in a corner reading a book. He got to know her, and he was so impressed by her intelligence and achievement that he secured for her a scholarship to Nicolet, a private high school in a wealthy suburb twenty-five miles from her mother's home.

She was the only black student at Nicolet, yet she became the most popular girl in the school, at least partly because the other kids were trying to show off their recently acquired racial broad-mindedness. Oprah visited their homes, and although she was grateful for acceptance, she soon realized what it was like to live in a "real" family while seeing herself, in contrast, as an "ugly, poor girl." She soon became rebellious—lying, stealing money from her mother's purse, and "dating everything with pants on." Vernita forbade Oprah to have anything to do with boys (although she herself was gallivanting every night). Her mother's rules notwithstanding, at age fourteen, Oprah became pregnant, but her premature infant died shortly after. Unable to cope with her, her mother finally sent her back to Vernon and Zelma.

Vernon was then the owner of a combination barbershop-grocery in a friendly, mostly black neighbor-hood of Nashville. He also acted as deacon in the Faith-United Church. Vernon took on a stronger role as father: he demanded of Oprah an 11 p.m. curfew, no makeup, no halter tops, and no miniskirts. "Listen, girl," he used to say, "if I tell you a mosquito can pull a wagon, don't ask me no questions. Just hitch him up." Every two weeks Zelma took Oprah to the library for five books, on which she was required to write reports for her parents. During this time Oprah discovered Maya Angelou's moving *I Know Why the Caged Bird Sings*, detailing Angelou's own account of her childhood sexual abuse. Oprah finally understood that her own victimization had never been her fault. She saw, too, that her self-indulgence in Milwaukee had really been a kind of self-imprisonment.

As a result of forced desegregation, Oprah was one of the first black students at East High in Nashville, and because of her positive experience at Nicolet, she was able to bridge the edgy gap between blacks and whites. She also performed dramatic readings of the life of indomitable black women like Harriet Tubman and Sojourner Truth. She easily won election as president of the student body and in 1970 was invited to represent her school at the White House Conference on Youth in Denver. At sixteen, she won the Tennessee state oratorical contest and a partial scholarship to Tennessee State. The following year Oprah entered a local beauty contest and made it to the final cut. When the three finalists were asked what each would do with a million dollars, the first girl said she would buy presents for her family, the girl second said she would give it to the poor, and Oprah, knowing all the "proper" answers were used up, said, "I'd be a spending fool!" She won hands down, and when she went to the sponsoring radio station to pick up her prizes, the management was so impressed with her intelligence and the depth and clarity of her voice, they gave her a job reading the news every half-hour from after school until evening.

In 1972, Oprah won the Miss Black Nashville and Miss Black Tennessee contests and a four-year scholarship to Tennessee State, along with an all-expenses trip to compete in the Miss Black America pageant in Hollywood. But she wasn't happy. Living at home while attending college was cramping. Oprah began to feel that beauty pageants were degrading to women, and she began to feel self-conscious about her dark skin and her weight. While at Tennessee State, she majored in drama (against Vernon's objections), starred in university plays, gave dramatic readings in local churches, and before she had finished her freshman year was offered a job as a television newscaster at the Nashville CBS affiliate, WTVF. She was a natural, easygoing and unthreatening. Viewers described her style as if "listening to gossip from a next-door neighbor."

In June 1976, at age twenty-two, Oprah was offered a job hosting a talk show in Baltimore. She had found her niche: "I came off the air, and I knew that was what I was supposed to do. It just felt like breathing." After six years, she moved to *A.M. Chicago* at a salary of $200,000. She knew absolutely no one in Chicago, so she spent her first Christmas working in a soup kitchen for street people.

Oprah may not have known many people in Chicago, but she was gaining attention nationally. *Newsweek* devoted a full page to her and she made her first appearance on *The Tonight Show*. By her second year in Chicago, *A.M. Chicago* became *The Oprah Winfrey Show*. More offers followed. Stephen Spielberg offered her the part of the tough-as-nails Sofia in the film of Alice Walker's *The Color Purple*, the story of strong, poor black women whose courage and fundamental self-respect ennobled them—despite sexual abuse, bullying males, racial cruelty, and, in Sofia's case, police brutality. Oprah fitted into Sofia's soul like an apple into its skin. She was nominated for an Oscar for Best Supporting Actress.

When *The Oprah Winfrey Show* went into syndication, it became the highest-ranked talk show in the country. When Oprah plugged a book on her show, it would lodge itself on the best-seller lists for months. She formed HARPO ("Oprah" spelled backward) Productions to develop films, documentaries, and television movies to raise the American consciousness. Of her talk show, she said, "What we are trying to tackle in this one hour is what I think is the root of all the problems in the world—lack of self-esteem." Addressing the Tennessee State graduation class in 1987, Oprah said, "Don't complain about what you don't have. Use what you've got. To do less than your best is a sin. Every single one of us has the power of greatness, because greatness is determined by service—to yourself and to others."

When you *make* good, something good in you impels you to *do* good.

Points to Ponder

1. It might be hard to believe, but if you can read this page, you are genuinely *gifted*. Nearly 44 million adults in the United States can't read a newspaper or fill out a job application. Another 50 million *more* can't read or comprehend above the eighth grade level. That's nearly half of all American adults. How do you feel about reading? Is there something rebellious inside you that *resents* being pushed to read ever-more-challenging books? Given the competitive nature of our world (not to mention personal pride), how could anyone resist sharpening reading skills?

2. Objectively, you're also amazingly more gifted than all humans if you count on three meals today, see a doctor every few years, or are confident of living beyond age seventy-five. Since you started this page, about two hundred people died of starvation; by the end of the year four million more will. If every person in Tanzania saw a doctor yearly, each MD would have to treat 20,000; in Chad, 28,000, in Rwanda, 50,000. The average world life expectancy is sixty-seven; in Nigeria, forty-seven; in Swaziland, forty. This is not to make you feel guilty, just grateful. Does owning

those truths at least make it more difficult to grumble, "Tuna casserole and broccoli *again*?"

3. Oprah displays a bewildering kind of gratitude to people who might unhesitatingly cramp her freedom, limit her choices, or impose their will on hers. Can you explain why she values these kinds of people so much? Do you think she ranks what is important in life differently from what most people settle for? Do you think she is better off or worse off for her life-view?

three

●●●●●●

Helen Keller

●●●●●●●●●●●●●

Author, Activist, Lecturer

1880–1968

Curiosity:

Pronunciation: \kyur-ē-ä-s(ə)tē\
Function: *noun*
Date: 14th century
1: desire to know: **a:** inquisitive interest in others'
concerns: nosiness **b:** interest leading to inquiry

◇◇◇

The important thing is not to stop questioning. Curiosity
has its own reason for existing. One cannot help
but be in awe when he contemplates the mysteries of
eternity, of life, of the marvelous structure of reality.
—Albert Einstein

◇◇◇

Where can I hide from your spirit?
From your presence, where can I flee?
If I ascend to the heavens, you are there;
if I lie down in Sheol, you are there too.
If I fly with the wings of dawn
and alight beyond the sea,
Even there your hand will guide me,
your right hand hold me fast.
If I say, "Surely darkness shall hide me,
and night shall be my light"—
Darkness is not dark for you,
and night shines as the day.
Darkness and light are but one.

—Psalm 139:7–12

Fifteen years after the Civil War, Helen Keller was born in Tuscumbia, Alabama, the third child of Captain Arthur Keller, a former Confederate officer, wealthy landowner, and newspaper publisher; and his second wife, Kate. The family adored the baby, but at nineteen months, Helen fell victim to a mysterious illness doctors now believe was scarlet fever. When the fever finally broke, the family rejoiced, but almost immediately realized something was terribly wrong. The baby girl slept poorly, almost as if she were smothering in frustration, and she constantly hid her face from light. Finally, the doctors realized that Helen's eyes and ears were sealed forever.

As she grew older and stronger, Helen became more difficult. Her moods swung from despondency to fierce anger. Some of those who observed her thought she was so simple-minded that she should be institutionalized.

What's more, her unpredictable moods and behavior became dangerous to others. One time, finding her baby sister sleeping in her own doll's cradle and incapable of knowing what it was, Helen overturned the cradle. Fortunately their mother was there to catch the baby. As Helen's inner intelligence grew, so did her frustrations, like a child in a straitjacket in an airless room.

Without any help from outside, she nonetheless began to use signs to make her feelings and demands known: a shake of the head meant "No," a nod "Yes," a pull "Come," a shove "Go away." If Helen was hungry, she mimicked cutting bread; if she wanted her father, she pretended to put on glasses; if she wanted her mother, she pulled her hair into a knot at the back of her head. By age five, she had a "vocabulary" of about sixty gestures—and all of this with no more input than what she'd been able to ingest as a child of a year and a half, before the darkness.

Imagine what Helen's life was like without color and without tones. She could contact only surfaces and vibrations with her hands. She knew by the smells and textures when she was in the house—but she didn't know it *was* a house. She'd worked out a safe path through it, a dark little world where she could remember where harmful objects were. Outside was different, too big to plot a safe path through it. When she felt the soft thing under her feet (which was the grass), every step she took was taken in fear, because the next step could be the edge of everything.

She was the only *person* in her dark, little world. Others were just bodies. She was utterly alone, and everything else was enemy—dark, unseen, always threatening. But inside this girl was a fierce intelligence, agonizing to break free, like a ship trapped in impenetrable fog.

Helen's mother had never given up hope for her daughter. Reading a book of Charles Dickens's notes on his travels in America, she found an item describing his meeting a girl named Laura Bridgman, blind and deaf from a very young age, who had learned to communicate at the Perkins Institution in Boston. Meanwhile, a Baltimore eye specialist suggested Helen visit Washington, D.C., to see Alexander Graham Bell, whose telephone had come about from his efforts to teach deaf children.

Bell invited Captain Keller and Helen to dinner, and he warmed to her immediately. "He understood my signs," Helen wrote later, "and I knew it and loved him at once. But I did not dream that interview would be the door through which I would pass from darkness into light, from isolation to friendship, companionship, knowledge, and love." Bell also suggested that Helen go to Perkins.

Captain Keller wrote to the Perkins Institution, pleading for a teacher for Helen. The teacher assigned was twenty-one-year-old Annie Sullivan, abandoned by her immigrant Irish parents at age nine and sent to the Massachusetts poorhouse in Tewksbury. There Annie had spent five years with the castoffs of society: alcoholics, the helpless elderly, and the insane. Almost blind from an eye disease she contracted when she was very young, Annie was illiterate until age fourteen, when Perkins accepted her. After enduring surgeries and education over the next six years, she had most of her sight restored and graduated first in her class. Annie spent many hours with the aging Laura Bridgman, still at Perkins, and from her she learned the secret, silent, lonely place Laura had wandered in so long.

When Annie arrived in Tuscumbia on March 3, 1887, she carried in her case a doll for Helen that the Perkins students had pooled their allowances to buy, clad in doll clothes made by Laura Bridgman. Annie met a near-savage child with wild hair, who swung her fists against Annie's attempt to embrace her. When her mother stopped Helen from grabbing Annie's purse, Helen rocked and howled on the floor. "There is nothing pale or delicate about

Helen," Annie wrote to a friend at Perkins. "She is large, strong, and ruddy, and as unrestrained in her movements as a young colt."

But in the middle of Helen's tantrum, Annie handed her a pocket watch, and the girl calmed, feeling it with her fingers, her empty eyes signaling puzzlement. Somehow, her inaccessible mind intuited watches had something to do with time, and that there would be candy later. Helen was excruciatingly curious, which is the only place from which any true learning can begin.

On the next morning, Annie began. First she spelled "doll" in Helen's hand, then put the doll from the Perkins children in her hands. Helen went along, mimicking the word, but with no idea she was spelling, or even that words existed. She was simply imitating and had little or no comprehension. When she grew bored, she batted Annie's hands away, then hurled the new doll, smashing it to pieces. A couple of weeks later, Helen punched out two of Annie's teeth.

No one had ever made much effort to curb the child. Whatever Helen wanted, she got. If she refused to be cleaned up, they allowed it; at meals, she pawed anything she wanted from anyone's plate, but one morning when Helen grabbed food from Annie's plate, Annie slapped her hand. Shocked, Helen tried again, and got another slap. The Kellers were furious, but Annie simply ushered them all out of the dining room and locked the door. Helen lay on the floor, kicking and screaming, trying to pull Annie's chair out from under her. Helen then pinched Annie, and Annie slapped her in return every time. Helen felt her way around the table and knew they were alone. After a few minutes, she returned to her place and began to eat her breakfast with her fingers.

Captain Keller bristled at Annie's discipline but reluctantly began to see that, without control, all Annie's work would be useless. So Annie and Helen moved into a small cottage on the farm and gradually began to know one another. Slowly, Helen began to associate Annie with "home," with something (not yet "someone") reliable. Helen found it more pleasant to be clean rather dirty. She learned that when she was willing to eat with a spoon, Annie would provide her food. And always there was that strange game in the palm of her hand. Whenever she held her doll, four funny signs; whenever she got a glass of water, five funny signs. That's all it was, just a game.

Then one day it happened. Helen was impatient and angry at her lesson, so Annie took her for a walk, out in the yard, near the pump. She hit the pump and shoved Helen's hands into the water, writing the word "water" in her other hand. Something inside the girl was beginning to connect; something choked into her throat. And from her twisted mouth came the only word she could remember from her babyhood, before the darkness: "Wa-wa."

It had happened. The invasion. Helen had discovered things have names. There was a world beyond her darkness, and—even though she couldn't see them—there were other *persons*, like her, people who could communicate to her through the strange game in her hand. Poor frightened girl. She'd made the most liberating of all human discoveries: She wasn't alone.

In an ecstasy of understanding, Helen breathlessly touched the pump, her tugging hand begging its name. Then the trellis, the well house itself. By the end of the day, Helen had learned thirty words, but most important, she knew what they *meant!* In their walks after, she was relentless to know everything she contacted: eggs, chickens, piglets, flowers, puppies, a dead squirrel. Within three *months*, Helen accumulated over three hundred words, and Annie decided it was time to read Braille. She spelled each letter in Helen's hand, then touched her fingertips to the nubbly raised letter embossed on a card. In just one day, Helen learned the whole Braille alphabet! "When her finger lights upon words she knows, she fairly screams with pleasure, hugs and kisses me for joy."

By June of 1887, only three months after Annie had first come to Tuscumbia, Helen had learned to write, using a board marked with deep horizontal lines, guiding her right hand with her left. Annie rejoiced in Helen's joy and her restlessly inquisitive mind. In November, Helen went to her first circus, and the performers let her feel and feed the elephants. She stroked the lion cubs; a leopard licked her hand; a big black bear offered her his paw. When she kissed all the circus performers in grinning gratitude, some of them wept.

At age eight, Helen went with her mother and Annie to Boston to visit the Perkins School. "What a joy to talk to other children in my own language!" The library held the country's largest collection of Braille books, and Helen's fingers scampered over the raised dots, hungry for more. She also met Laura Bridgman, the woman who "bridged the chasm between mankind and me."

Helen soon learned to sculpt, she dabbled in French and Greek, and her English fluency was astonishing: eighty words a minute. Then, she spelled in Annie's hands: "I must speak." So Annie took her to Sarah Fuller, principal of Boston's Horace Mann School for the Deaf, and Fuller painstakingly taught Helen by allowing her to feel her mouth as she formed words. Within an hour she could pronounce six sounds. After ten lessons she was able to gargle to Annie: "I am not dumb now." She never learned to speak clearly, but Sarah Fuller taught her to lip-read by touching the lips and throats of the speaker. She learned to "hear" music the same way.

Because of her father's failing businesses, Helen's chances of further education—or even a continued salary for Annie—looked bleak, but through the pleas of Alexander Graham Bell and Mark Twain, enough money was accumulated to send Helen first to the Cambridge School for Young Ladies, where she interacted easily with ordinary young women, and then to a private tutor so that, at age nineteen, she was prepared to take the entrance examination for Radcliffe College.

Despite Radcliffe's initial reluctance, Helen was admitted. Annie went along with her. Helen's biggest challenge was to rush home after classes to transcribe into Braille what she could remember of Annie's fingered communications of the lectures. In 1902, *The Ladies' Home Journal*, offered Helen $3,000 for her life story, an amount she was hardly able to turn down. The following year, when Helen was only twenty-three, *The Story of My Life* appeared as a book, to enthusiastic reviews. Eventually, it was translated into fifty languages.

Helen was restless, tired of writing about only one subject: herself. She became interested in the plight of the poor, women's rights, economics, politics, and pacifism. Many thought her impertinent. Who was she to write about complex subjects? Always in search of money to survive, she and Annie toured the country giving "lectures." When Annie became ill, Helen finally accepted an annuity from Andrew Carnegie, which allowed them to hire an assistant, Polly Thompson, to take care of their housekeeping and finances.

In three years, Helen and Annie toured 123 cities, raising more than a million dollars for the blind, a mind-boggling amount in the 1920s. She captivated presidents from Grover Cleveland to Lyndon Johnson, as well as the great figures of her age like Enrico Caruso, Jascha Heifitz, Maria Montessori, Henry Ford, Eleanor Roosevelt, and Charlie Chaplin.

In 1936, Annie Sullivan, then nearly blind herself, died. Her last words were, "Thank God I gave up my life that Helen might live." Friends wondered if Helen could survive, but with Polly Thompson, she continued to write and lecture, campaigning for blind workers. During World

War II, she toured military hospitals, encouraging soldiers who had been blinded or deafened in battle. After the war, she toured thirty-five countries, promoting programs for the disabled.

Helen died peacefully on June 1, 1968, at the age of eighty-eight. She had moved from utter loneliness in the dark to a rich, full life, known and respected by millions because her restless mind and fingers refused to yield. As Helen said, "Life is either a daring adventure or nothing."

Points to Ponder

1. Babies are born chock-full of curiosity, their eyes and fingers exploring every waking moment. Wise parents rise to that challenge, surrounding infants with bright-colored, shiny, musical toys to keep that life-giving sense of wonder alive. In fact, nerve specialists have shown that in a child *deprived* of such stimuli, brain cells actually wither and permanently die. You can probably remember times when you were young when even an empty box stirred your imagination. Nowadays you are often surrounded by the slack jaws and dulled eyes of boredom. What was lost?

2. Before her great insight, Helen Keller believed she was the only person in the world—the only one with feelings, frustrations, angry reactions to intrusions. Is it possible that you have your own unnatural resistances to other human beings who could otherwise enrich your life? What would an Annie Sullivan have to do to convince you to crack open your secure, self-centered world and let the great world come flooding in?

3. The innermost core of the advertising industry, which has formed our values since infancy, is the message that "more is better!"—more impressive schooling, more pay, and more

youth. Helen Keller was motivated by the same insatiable hunger, but how were the *goals* of her hunger different from those of most people today? And what did those goals do to Helen's inmost self that today's advertising values don't seem to satisfy?

four

••••

César Chávez

•••••••••••••••

Farm Worker, Labor Leader, Civil Rights Activist

1927–1993

Responsibility:

Pronunciation: \ri-spän(t)-sə-bi-lə-tē\
Function: *noun*
Date: 1737
1: the quality or state of being responsible: as **a:** moral,
legal, or mental accountability **b:** reliability, trustworthiness
2: something for which one is responsible: burden

◇◇◇

If you're not part of the solution, you're part of the problem.
—Eldridge Cleaver

◇◇◇

Then I heard the voice of the Lord saying, "Whom shall I send?
Who will go for us?" "Here I am," I said; "send me!"
—Isaiah 6:8

37

One week it was picking lettuce at a farm in central California. Who knew where they would be the next week and what the job would be? From the time he was only ten, César, his parents, and his siblings woke every morning at 3 a.m. to meet the labor contractor, whose bus rattled them along dusty roads to work the fields until 4 p.m., when they would rattle back to a one-room shack in some labor camp. It only had one light bulb, no furniture, and no water. In a week of twelve-hour days, the family hoped to make $20, barely enough after the shack rental and food to bus them a hundred miles north to the next agricultural valley, following the crops. The next week it might be picking fruit. Much better than working with the short hoe that bent your backbone like a bow too tightly strung. One thing César could be sure of: You can be sure of nothing.

César Estrada Chávez was born in Yuma, Arizona, on March 31, 1927. During the Depression, his father, Librado, ran a grocery store, an auto repair shop, and a poolroom twenty miles north of Yuma. César learned from his mother never to turn away anyone who came to their house in need of food, and there were many ordinary people who did seek help from his family. Ironically, most who needed assistance were the Anglos, though Anglo children at school called César and the other Chicanos "dirty Mexicans," mocked their accents, and took any chance to bully them.

Librado had overextended himself and, worse, gave credit to too many friends and relatives strapped for cash. The family was finally penniless, so in August of 1937, when César was ten, the family crowded into their old car and headed for California in hope of work. The Chávez family soon found that California was paradise only for the rich. Labor contractors often owned the camps where the migrants lived in tents or tarpaper shacks, deducting workers' rent from their pay at exorbitant rates and charging inflated prices for supplies at the camp store. They over-recruited workers and then lowered the wage promised. They charged Social Security and then pocketed the proceeds. There was corruption at all levels of the operation.

In 1944, at age seventeen, César joined the Navy, but two years later he was back in the fields. In October 1948, he married Helen Fabela. They eventually would have eight children. The family settled in the Mexican barrio of San Jose, California, called *Sal Si Puedes* ("Get out if you can"), where César finally found a more secure, full-time job working in a lumberyard. In *Sal Si Puedes*, César Chávez came face to face with his destiny.

The pastor of the barrio church was Fr. Thomas McDonnell. He was sent by the Archdiocese of San Francisco to work with farm laborers, visit the camps, minister to the workers' spiritual needs, and make them aware of Church teachings on social justice and labor. He gave César the papal encyclicals on labor, books on labor history, and Louis Fisher's *Life of Gandhi*. César was so impressed by the life and work of that ascetic messiah of nonviolent protest that he went on to read anything he could find about him. Gandhi preached of self-discipline and the need for complete sacrifice of oneself for others.

Another significant influence on César was Fred Ross, an organizer in San Jose for Saul Alinsky's Community Service Organization (CSO), established to help Mexican Americans organize and exert a unified pressure on those individuals and institutions that exploited them. The CSO focused on issues in the urban barrios: civil rights violations, voter registration, community action, education, and housing. "As time went on, Fred became sort of my hero. I saw him organize, and I wanted to learn," César recalled.

César began working full-time for Ross at a salary of $50 a week. His first job was to get to know people and help with their needs, then to expect those he helped to become helpers themselves. "You must become a servant of the people. When you do, you can demand their commitment in return." From the modest dues ($3.50 a month) in César's own newly established Farm Workers' Association (later the United Farm Workers), he and Helen set up a credit union from which members could borrow in emergencies. Helen became its administrator, working out of the garage of their cheap rental home in nearby Delano. He found his most important source of support came from ordinary, poor workers, not from the middle class, who were at best suspicious of him and at worst branded him a Communist for inciting unrest among the poor. His most potent means of calling attention to inhuman treatment were boycotts, marches, and political lobbying. Meanwhile, César was reading anything he could find on labor organizations and came to two critical realizations: Don't try to do two things at once, and organize *before* you think of strikes.

Gradually, the Farm Workers' Association drew in others as single-mindedly dedicated as themselves, among them Rev. Jim Drake, a Protestant minister, and the woman destined to be César's alter ego, Dolores Huerta, a housewife with small children who was just completing her college degree on the way to becoming an indispensable lobbyist. César's cousin, Manuel, designed the Association's flag: a fierce black eagle symbolizing the workers' brutal situation, emerging from a white circle of hope, surrounded by a blood-red field signifying what justice cost. Their motto: *Sí, Se Puede* ("Yes, it can be done").

But it could not be done easily. Members who originally signed up soon lost interest or courage, or needed the $3.50 for more pressing needs. Finally, César hit on a method of recruitment: hold a barbecue with free food, but beverages for sale to pay for costs and sign up anyone who attended. By 1964, the union had a thousand dues-paying members and more than fifty local chapters.

The critical moment came in early 1965, in Delano. Laborers had been brought in from Mexico to work even more cheaply than the local Filipino and Mexican Americans at the Schenley vineyards. César called a meeting. The hall filled with blacks, Puerto Ricans, Filipinos, Arabs, Anglos, and Mexicans, shouting, "*Huelga!* Strike!" Picketers lined the roads outside vineyards, trying to cajole the scabs to join them instead of taking their jobs. Company foremen raced pickups along the roads, choking picketers with dust and spraying them with pesticides. The police never intervened.

But picketers found the point beyond which no human could allow himself to be degraded. "When a man or woman takes a place on a picket line for even a day or two," César said, "they will never be the same again. They have confirmed their humanity. Through non-violence, they have confirmed the humanity of others. . . . We can turn the world, if we can do it nonviolently. We will not let ourselves be provoked by our adversaries into behaving hatefully. We draw our strength from the very despair in which we have been forced to live. We shall endure."

César went to California college campuses to recruit volunteers, not with wild rhetoric, but with the example of sincerity, humility, and searingly objective facts about dehumanization. An NBC special mounted by Fred Friendly and Edward R. Murrow, *Harvest of Shame*, focused the attention of the entire country on the farm workers' anguish. Walter Reuther, head of the United Auto Workers, pledged his support. César organized a 250-mile march from Delano to the state capitol in Sacramento. Hundreds joined them along the way; by the time they reached Stockton, they were five thousand, singing, chanting, and waving. Then, in April, when news came that

New York bartenders refused to sell Schenley products, the major employer gave way and agreed to a contract.

But in the late 1960s, America had become a snake pit of resentments—over the Vietnam War, racial injustice, and government's toadying to vested interests. California governor Ronald Reagan appeared on television urging viewers to ignore the boycott and support the growers. President Richard Nixon ordered the Defense Department to send two million pounds of grapes to Vietnam. The mood of violent response to injustice spread to the UFW, and César had to go up and down picket lines taking weapons away from angry picketers. Finally, he declared publicly that he would begin a fast, as Gandhi had done, until his followers had firmly recommitted themselves to nonviolence. The fast lasted twenty-five days and ended with a Catholic Mass for four thousand workers. It was covered by the national media. On July 20, 1970, twenty-nine grape growers assembled near Delano to sign union contracts with the UFW, giving a wage of $1.80 per hour plus ten cents an hour to the workers' health fund.

But when UFW's table-grape agreements came up for renegotiation in 1973, the growers signed with the Teamsters Union, prompting ten thousand farm workers in California's valleys to walk out of the fields in protest. César called for a worldwide wine and grape boycott, and by 1975 a Harris poll showed 17 million American adults were honoring it. More than fifteen thousand people followed César on a 110-mile march from San Francisco to the Gallo winery in Modesto, and in May the California Agricultural Labor Relations Act was the first law governing farm labor approved in the continental United States. Dues-paying membership of UFW soared to one hundred thousand.

In the 1980s, UFW produced a film, *The Wrath of Grapes*, citing with graphic footage a high number of birth defects among farm workers along with statistics that the conditions were due to close proximity to pesticides. In July 1988, César began a fast to protest pesticides, during which he consumed only water. Dolores Huerta warned reporters, "This is a spiritual thing for him. This is not a publicity stunt." It lasted thirty-six days. Eugene Nelson described the kind of person who would do such things: "a man with a healthy sense of his own worth and with a corresponding intense drive to see that he and his kind are treated as equals; yet, he has a disarming simplicity, down-to-earthiness, and interest in the ordinary things of life." Like other UFW officers and staff, he never made more than $5,000 a year.

"There has to be someone who is willing to do it," César said. "There has to be someone who is willing to take whatever risks are required. I don't think it can be done with money alone. The person has to be dedicated to the task. . . . I am convinced that the truest act of courage, the strongest act of humanity, is to sacrifice ourselves for others in a totally nonviolent struggle for justice. To be human is to suffer for others." Luis Solis-Garza put it well: "He had a fire inside him."

César Chávez died in his sleep April 23, 1993, at the age of sixty-six. At his funeral in Delano a week later, thirty-five thousand people from all over the world gathered to honor him. His twenty-seven grandchildren went up to the coffin together and laid on it a carving of the UFW eagle and a short-handled hoe.

Points to Ponder

1. Why do you think César Chávez was concerned with the needs of others beyond the obvious needs of his own family? What led him to give more of his life? Edmund Burke wrote, "All that is needed for the triumph of evil is that good people be silent." Does humility at some times cease to be virtuous? Why is saying, "Oh, I'm nobody," usually a self-fulfilling prophecy?

2. What do you think are the benefits of unionizing workers? Sometimes unions have such a stranglehold on the public with the threat of crippling strikes that their power is a civic menace. What is your honest assessment of workers' unions?

3. Think of something that *really* bothers you in your neighborhood, your city, or your country. Is that inequity something at least potentially curable? Get a tight focus on a single real goal which is doable for someone in your situation. Now what will you do?

five

····

Anne Frank

···············

Author, Holocaust Victim

1929–1945

Hope:

Pronunciation: \hōp\
Function: *verb*
Etymology: Middle English, from Old English *hopian*;
akin to Middle High German *hoffen* to hope
Date: before 12th century
intransitive verb
1: to cherish a desire with anticipation
2 *archaic:* trust
transitive verb
1: to desire with expectation of obtainment
2: to expect with confidence: trust

◇◇◇

Once you choose hope, anything's possible.
—Christopher Reeve

◇◇◇

For creation was made subject to futility, not of its own accord
but because of the one who subjected it, in hope that creation
itself would be set free from slavery to corruption and share in
the glorious freedom of the children of God.

—Romans 8:20–21

Once the workers arrived in the offices and warehouse below at 8:30 a.m., there had to be dead silence. The eight Jews in the attic rooms of 263 Prinsengracht on a busy Amsterdam canal had all risen from their narrow beds at 6:45, shoved them out of the way, lined up for a quick cold-water wash and breakfast. Then they had to withdraw within themselves, to study, to sew or knit, or to pore over business files until 12:30, when the warehouse closed for lunch. Then they could sneak down to the office bathroom, where they could use the flush toilet instead of the embarrassing bucket. An eerie world of tedium and tension, especially for thirteen-year-old Anne Frank, who wrote in her diary, "It seems to me that neither I—nor for that matter anyone else—will be interested in the disclosures of a thirteen-year-old schoolgirl. Still, what does that matter? I want to write, but more than that, I want to bring out all kinds of things that lie buried deep in my heart." And that she did, utterly unaware she would be a focal figure in twentieth-century history.

Anne had no notion her diary would be the eighth most widely read book ever published. Nor that those attic rooms in Holland would draw eight hundred thousand visitors every year. Nor that *Time* magazine would say that the writing of a precocious adolescent girl captured "the moral individual mind, beset by the machinery of destruction, insisting on the right to live and question and hope for the future of human beings."

In February 1934, when Annaliese Frank was not quite four and her sister, Margot, was seven, their parents, Otto and Edith Frank, moved the family from Frankfurt, Germany, to Amsterdam because of the increasing intensity of Nazi power and fierce oppression against the Jews. Even though Otto won the Iron Cross in the German army in World War I and only Edith really practiced Judaism, Hitler presumed Jews' bloodlines were as contaminated as if they were werewolves to be eliminated. In Amsterdam, Otto set up a spice business with Hermann van Pels, his expert blender.

For eight years, from 1934 to 1942, the Franks lived the lives of an ordinary assimilated Jewish family, going to school, entertaining Christian and Jewish friends, and waiting for the business to find its feet. Margot was well-mannered, restrained, and good at studies; Anne was assertive, lively, and extroverted. Anne's diary, begun in 1942, evidences a quick, incisive mind, sharp, confident observations, and uncommon (for an adolescent), intense honesty with herself, about herself. (However, after the war, her father excised pages from the diary that could have easily been misread as too touchy, vain, unfair, or jealous. As a result, the play and films based on her life make her seem like some disembodied saint, whereas she was really an ordinary girl.) She was pert, impish, not above batting her eyelashes to get her way, and more than comfortable as the center of attention. Like any girl her age, she wanted to be taken seriously, not to be treated like a baby, and yet at the same time wanted to be cuddled and spoiled.

But the world was closing in on their lack of drama and contentment. Germany slowly devoured most of central Europe, and though Hitler swore to respect the neutral countries, he had proved time and again that for him "swear" and "respect" were merely words. At dawn, Friday, May 10, 1940, with no declaration, Germany invaded Holland to "protect" it from British invasion. By the following Friday, Holland surrendered.

At first, the anti-Jewish laws were merely irritating— things like exclusion from movies, beaches, and parks, but the next wave of laws against Jews came with prohibitions from working and from riding in trams, cars, and even on bicycles. In September 1941, Jewish children were restricted to separate schools. Things got worse: Jews were required to wear a star patch on all their clothing, and in June 1942, all Jews were registered for possible deportation to labor camps in Germany. Then in the early summer of 1942, fifteen-year-old Margot Frank received a summons to report for transport.

In anticipation of intensifying German persecution, the Franks had been preparing four tiny rooms hidden behind a swinging bookcase on the top two floors of the Prinsen-gracht building, where the ground floor was a warehouse and the second floor offices. Otto had already had his busi-ness reincorporated in the names of his trusted Gentile employees, Victor Kugler and Jan Gies. The two rooms on the third floor were little wider than their windows, along with a cold-water sink and bucket toilet. The larger of the two was the parents' bedroom, the smaller Anne and Margot's. Above was the common room with a table, coal stove, a sink, and a kitchen cabinet, which had been the company's spice lab. Squeezed into a corner on that floor was the smallest room, wide enough only for a camp bed and the stairs up to the cramped attic. Up there at night, peering through the blackout curtains, the prisoners could see the face of the clock at Westkirk church, where the great Rembrandt was buried, and listen to the mournful notes of its bells.

Very early on July 6, 1942, the family left their home for the so-called "Secret Annex," laden with suitcases and wearing three sets of clothes. Anne's priorities in packing were not typical of a teenage girl; the first item was her diary: "Memories are more important to me than dresses." In the annex, they began what they didn't suspect would be two years of seclusion. As Anne wrote, it seemed at first little more than "a vacation in a very peculiar boarding house." Beyond the suppressed resentments every family must deal with, the Franks' sensitivities suffered further when, later that month, they were joined by Otto's business partner, Hermann van Pels, his argumentative wife, Auguste, and their sixteen-year-old son, Peter, whom Anne found at first shy, awkward, and a total bore. The tensions grew with the addition in November of a fifty-four-year-old dentist, Fritz Pfeffer, whom Anne describes as "stodgy, old-fashioned, preachy, and small-minded." And he snored.

As the months grated onward, suppressing the antagonisms under rigid politeness became more and more nerve-racking.

At least some easement came each evening when the workers had left and the refugees could come cautiously into the relative openness of the offices on the second floor to listen to the forbidden BBC, exercise, even take sponge baths in real hot water. They had always to be cautious of showing any light or making any sound, careful never to leave any trace of their presence behind, but they could never be perfect. One time a warehouseman found the wallet that slipped out of Pfeffer's pocket. On another occasion a cleaning woman was sure she had heard noises overhead. It took the best skill at deception on the part of the Franks' non-Jewish friends to fend them off.

Anne's diary would have been unheard and unpublished without the heroic assistance provided by Otto's associates and employees, especially his partner Jan Gies and Jan's wife, Miep. During their captivity, Jan and Miep supplied the food (in part by ordering extra bread for their employees) and, equally as important, all the news from the outside world. After the Franks' arrest, Miep rescued Anne's diary. Clearly these brave people did what they did simply because of who they *were*.

Since that time, the world has fastened on Anne Frank's story not just because it embodies the absolute insanity of the Nazis' persecution of the Jews, but because Anne herself captures the resilience of the human spirit. In her smothering captivity, she wrote:

> It's difficult in times like these: ideals, dreams and cherished hopes rise within us only to be crushed by grim reality. It's a wonder I haven't abandoned all my ideals, they seem so absurd and impractical. Yet I cling to them because I still believe, in spite of everything, that people are truly good at heart. . . . It's utterly impossible for me to build my life on a foundation of chaos, suffering and death. I see the world being slowly transformed into a wilderness, I hear the approaching thunder [Allied bombing] that, one day, will destroy us too, I feel the suffering of millions. And yet, when I look up at the sky, I somehow feel that everything will change for the better, that this cruelty too shall end, that peace and tranquility will return once more. In the meantime, I must hold on to my ideals. Perhaps the day will come when I'll be able to realize them!

In January 1944, Anne wondered in a diary entry:

> Can you tell me why people go to such lengths to hide their real selves? Or why I always behave very differently when I'm in

the company of others? Why do people have so little trust in one another? I know there must be a reason, but sometimes I think it's horrible that you can't ever confide in anyone, not even those closest to you.

It's twice as hard for us young ones to hold our ground, in a time when all ideals are being shattered and destroyed, when people are showing their worst side, and do not know whether to believe in truth and right and in God.

Remember, these words are from a girl of fifteen, deprived of friends, romance, dancing, and sunshine. But not hope.

On the morning of August 4, 1944, in a violent clash with the hopes raised by the Allied invasion of France, the Annex was stormed by the German Security Police following a tip-off from an informant who was never identified. By August 8, the family was on a train to Westerbork, a camp through which one hundred thousand Dutch Jews had already passed. After four weeks, on September 3, the group was deported on what would be the last transport from Westerbork to the Auschwitz concentration camp—only one day before the Allies liberated Brussels. They arrived after three days' journey and were separated by sex. Of 1,019 passengers, 549—including all children younger than fifteen—were shunted directly to the gas chambers. Anne was not one of those. She had turned fifteen three months earlier.

On October 28, more than eight thousand women were relocated to the Bergen-Belsen camp in northwest Germany, including Anne, Margot, and Auguste van Pels, but not Edith Frank. Tents were erected in that muddy moonscape to accommodate the influx of prisoners. Then, in March 1945, a typhus epidemic raged through the camp killing some seventeen thousand prisoners. Witnesses later testified that Margot fell from her bunk and died of the shock, and a few days later Anne was dead, too, at age fifteen, just a few weeks before the camp was liberated by British troops on April 15, 1945. The camp had to be burned due to the contagion, and Anne and Margot were buried in a mass grave, the exact whereabouts unknown.

"Who has inflicted this on us?" Anne wrote just before her family was arrested. "Who has allowed us to suffer so terribly up 'til now? Is it God who made us as we are, but it will be God, too, who will raise us up again. If we bear all this suffering and if there are Jews left, when it is over, the Jews instead of being doomed will be held up as an example."

There are grating questions embedded in her cry. How could people who wouldn't kick their neighbors' dog treat fellow human beings like garbage? And what had the Jews done to "justify" such degradation? And what element within this innocent young girl clung relentlessly to her hope and to her conviction "that people are truly good at heart"?

Hannah Arendt, the Jewish political philosopher, argued against any supposed warped "cruel gene," or any disembodied devil, and proposed that the human susceptibility to evil comes from sheer banality—sheer *dullness* of spirit. As George tells Lenny in *Of Mice and Men*, it's not wicked people who cause all the pain. It's *dumb* people.

Points to Ponder

1. Imagine yourself locked for two years under the same oppressive conditions as the Franks—total wariness every minute, dependence on others, and, perhaps most taxing, the abrasive personalities of other people who grate on you to your very core. What in your everyday habits now could prepare you for such challenges? How can you steel yourself

right now to deal graciously with people you find unbearable? Explanation: If you look at life through bitter filters, it's amazing how many hateful people you'll find; but if you resolve to put on kindness filters, it's amazing how many of those hateful people seem more acceptable, worth at least giving a chance.

2. There's a huge difference between optimism and hope. Optimism—despite all the forbidding evidence—declares unreservedly that "the sun will come out tomorrow" and "everything will be just peachy!" Hope is more tentative: "I don't think I can do this. But I'll *try*." Amazingly, half the prisoners in Nazi extermination camps *did* survive. What kept them going was more than the sheer luck of a stronger physical constitution or the good luck not to contract disease. Try to focus what it was *within* those people that made them simply *refuse* to quit—despite unthinkable conditions. Eleanor Roosevelt said, "No one degrades you without your cooperation."

3. Sketch out a short story of an isolated society in which the well-to-do, handsome, athletic, and rich are not dominant but are, in fact, hunted, persecuted, shipped off to wilderness camps to work for people who in our present society are marginalized (e.g., the physically disabled or racially or religiously belittled). Think of films like *Planet of the Apes*. Then write a monologue in the words of one of the oppressed trying to explain what it feels like to be so dehumanized.

six

• • •

Jim Henson

• • • • • • • • • • •

Puppeteer, Director, Producer

1936–1990

Imagination:

Pronunciation: \i-ma-jə-nā-shən\
Function: *noun*
Etymology: Middle English, from Anglo-French, from
Latin *imagination-, imaginatio,* from *imaginari*
Date: 14th century
1: the act or power of forming a mental image of something not present to the senses or never before wholly
perceived in reality
2 a: creative ability **b:** ability to confront and deal with a
problem: resourcfulness **c:** the thinking or active mind:
interest
3 a: a creation of the mind; *especially*: an idealized or
poetic creation **b:** fanciful or empty assumption

◇◇◇

I saw the angel in the marble and carved till I set him free.
—Michelangelo

◇◇◇

Then afterward I will pour out
my spirit upon all mankind.
Your sons and daughter shall prophesy,
your old men shall dream dreams,
your young men shall see visions;
Even upon the servants and the handmaids,
in those days, I will pour out my spirit.

—Joel 3:1–2

J im Henson spent his first few years in Leland, Mississippi, where Deer Creek meanders through the town
toward the Mississippi River. It was a happy, Huck-
Finn time, swimming, fishing, daydreaming. He was in
his words "a quiet kid, introspective, articulate, always
involved with art, a fairly good student but a terrible
athlete." He was the kid coaches always stick out in right
field. But even way back then Jim was enthralled by fanciful characters, especially in movies like *The Wizard of Oz*.

Before 1950, there were few television sets. Radio
programming provided the same smorgasbord of choices
(news, soap operas, dramas, comedies, variety shows), but
with a difference: the listeners had to use their imaginations to supply the faces, the chases, and the places. So
Jim hunkered down by his radio, fleshing out superheroes,
detectives, and cowboys in his mind. One of his favorite
programs featured ventriloquist Edgar Bergen and his
dummies, wisecracking Charlie McCarthy and goofy Mor-
timer Snerd. "I don't ever remember thinking of them as
one man and his puppets. To me they were all human."

By the time he was in fifth grade, his father's work
took the family to Washington, D.C., where Jim slowly

adjusted to transplanting. But when television began to sprout and spread all over the country, Jim badgered his parents until they bought a family set when Jim was in the seventh grade. He fell in love with it, especially *Kukla, Fran, and Ollie*, a puppet show with Fran Allison as the human hostess, Kukla, a circus clown, and Ollie, a rather cuddly dragon—both worked by Burr Tillstrom, a puppeteer. In high school, Henson translated his interest and skill to making posters, drawing cartoons, and designing stage sets. He also joined with a group of kids interested in puppets. When he was seventeen, a local TV station advertised for a puppeteer for a morning children's show, so Jim and a friend whipped together three puppets—a French rat named Pierre and two cowboys named Longhorn and Shorthorn—and applied. They got the job, but they were dropped after three weeks. However, another local station, NBC affiliate WRC-TV, picked them up for the rest of the summer.

When Jim entered the University of Maryland to study acting, stagecraft, and scene design, he continued working at the station, and at the end of his freshman year, they offered him his own show, called *Sam and Friends*, a late-night filler packaged around a local show shot live and *The Tonight Show* with Steve Allen. As a partner to help with the puppets, Jim chose a classmate, Jane Nebel, because she had the same weird sense of humor, deft hands, and the ability to ad-lib situations. Their puppets didn't speak but would lip-sync to recordings while the characters cavorted and ended either by blowing up or gobbling up one another. One of his hand puppets was a green "thing" cut from Jim's mother's old coat with two halves of a ping-pong ball for eyes. Jim called him Kermit. He was supposed to be a lizard, but he evolved into a frog.

Jim used the frame of the television monitor as the model for a stage, and he and Jane stood under the screen with puppets raised over their heads, watching themselves on monitors so they could edit themselves as they went along. Steve Allen himself happened to see *Sam and Friends* one night and invited Jim and Jane onto *The Tonight Show*. Kermit, in a blond wig, sang "I've Grown Accustomed to Your Face" to a purple monster in a happy-face mask, after which Kermit proceeded to gobble him up—before the monster could do it first! Two years later, *Sam and Friends* won a Peabody Award for Best Local Entertainment Program, and Jim and Jane were married.

In 1960, when Jim went to his first puppeteers' convention in Detroit, he met Burr Tillstrom from *Kukla, Fran, and Ollie*, and they became lifelong friends. Tillstrom directed him to an agent named Bernie Brillstein, who took one look at Jim, this rangy, bearded guy in a loose shirt, jeans, and a headband and saw a "young Abe Lincoln wearing some kind of hippie arts-and-crafts clothes," but Brillstein decided he had better things to do with his time. But then he got word that Jim was signed into Radio City Music Hall, and Brillstein's priorities quickly rearranged themselves. They never signed a contract, but both were satisfied with a handshake that lasted thirty years as client and agent. Jim was honest, and he expected the same of everybody else.

When Jane retired to take care of what would become a family of five children, Jim went to California looking for new "Muppeteers" and met Jerry Juhl, who would become chief writer for all Jim's projects; Don Sahlin, a talented craftsman who made all his Muppets; and Frank Oz, just a sixteen-year-old kid at the time, who when he finished school joined Henson and went on to create Bert, Cookie Monster, Fozzie Bear, and, on the spur of the moment, the divine Miss Piggy.

Jim and Frank Oz were an inspired pair, the one quiet, the other exuberant, but their conversations were often marked by witty ad-libbing, which is how Miss Piggy (literally) came from the chorus to become an instant star.

While they were taping one day, Jim was operating Kermit while Frank worked a nameless female pig in a chorus of barnyard players, when suddenly on a whim Frank pushed his lady pig forward and burst into a solo, then turned and began to woo Kermit. A superstar was born. Oz kept probing Miss Piggy's character subtext to find her past filled with hardship, unyielding ambition to become a star, and a devouring lust for Kermit.

But their first star was Rowlf the Dog, whom country singer Jimmy Dean invited onto his show to play piano and sing duets with him. Rowlf's body was actually a hood covering two puppeteers, one to work the head and one arm, the second to work the other arm. Puppets with tiny arms were worked with wires on very thin rods, painted the same color as the background.

"The only way the magic works," Jim said, "is by hard work, but hard work can be fun." Muppets' jaws don't mimic every syllable, which would make big-mouthed figures look too agitated, and it took long practice to pick up the knack of mouthing the important syllables and usually a full year just to become reasonably good enough to work even background puppets. Operating a Muppet was like rubbing your head in one direction, your tummy in another, while tap dancing and singing, and the entire operation was, as Jim said, "a triumph of art over chaos."

The Muppets brought about a feeling of innocence and continue to do the same today. Jim explained the Muppets as "the simple-minded young person meeting life. Even the most worldly of our characters is innocent. Our villains are innocent, really. And it's that innocence that I think is the connection to the audience. The most sophisticated people I know—inside, they're all children. We never lose a certain sense we had when we were kids."

Perhaps Jim's biggest career break came when the Children's Television Workshop asked him to come up with ideas to help children, especially those in the inner city, prepare for school. Puppets were needed who could hold the children's attention and convey the way real kids feel facing real-life problems. Supported by human actors, cartoons, jingles, and stories, the objective was for puppets to teach children how to count and say their ABC's, but also to teach concepts like up, down, in, out. Thus, at Jim Henson's hands, on November 10, 1969, *Sesame Street*, an hour-long, daily program, was born on 179 public television stations across the country.

Jim's Muppets were from then on destined to be immortal, characters like Bert and Ernie, Cookie Monster, and Oscar the Grouch. Each Muppet ceased to be a piece of cloth and foam and a little wood and became a character that represented real-life children everywhere. Kermit, Jim said, is "an Everyman trying to get through life whole. He has a sense of sanity, and there he is, surrounded by crazies. He's the solid thing in the middle—flip, snarky, a bit smart-alecky, but a nice guy." Bert and Ernie quarrel, Oscar the Grouch is contrary, Miss Piggy is vain, the Great Gonzo is a hook-nosed creature unsure just what he is. All in all, the Muppets help children better understand themselves and their friends, which is what folktales have been doing for centuries. Probably the most important was Big Bird, a childlike Muppet Jim wanted to "stand in" for the average child in the audience—naïve while trying to figure out what was going on.

Sesame Street reminded everyone of an essential truth about learning: As long as learning is *intriguing*, it could be fun and easy. The show expanded beyond basic reading and math skills to deeper issues: childbirth, death, prejudice. In its first year, *Sesame Street* won a Peabody Award for Meritorious Service in Broadcasting, and every year after that it won more and more Emmys and other honors.

For years, Jim tried to convince network executives to back a regular Muppet evening series, but they kept insisting it was a children's show and that adults wouldn't watch. But after a few one-hour specials like "Hey, Cinderella" and "The Frog Prince," the British entrepreneur Lord Lew Grade decided to back Jim's idea. Thus was born *The Muppet Show*, a half-hour at the threshold of primetime, shot in England, with a celebrity guest each week. New characters began to appear, like the "oody-oody" Swedish chef and Stattler and Waldorf, two old fussbudgets who used to heckle the cast from a theater box. It was a wearying and chaotic schedule: taping twelve episodes of *The Muppet Show* in the summer, then a season's worth of *Sesame Street* in New York, then back to London, with scores of puppeteers and crew. But by the end of the third season, 235 million people followed *The Muppet Show* in over a hundred countries.

After *The Muppet Show* came *Fraggle Rock*, an underground world where feathery Fraggles coped with big shaggy Gorgs and tiny, round-headed Doozers, teaching children the lesson that, somehow, we have to get along with one another, no matter our differences. It was the first American television series allowed in what was then the Soviet Union.

Next, it was on to the big screen for Henson's crew. In 1979, *The Muppet Movie* was released. It showed the Muppets on their way to Hollywood, traveling in an old Studebaker. It took a lot of genius. In the opening scene, Kermit strums a banjo, sitting on a log in a real swamp. (Actually, Jim was in a tank sunk behind the log, moving Kermit's mouth and plucking with one arm while another puppeteer moved his other arm with an invisible wire fingering the frets.) All the regulars were in the car with two puppeteers each crammed beneath, while a little person drove the car from inside the trunk, with only a TV monitor to tell him what was ahead!

The success of his career and the accompanying stress continued for Jim into the 1980s. Then, in the spring of

1990, Jim had a sore throat and persistent fatigue. He thought it was flu. Then he began coughing blood. By the time he finally agreed to go to the hospital, he was diagnosed with a rare kind of pneumonia, and even with huge doses of antibiotics, the struggle was ultimately futile. He died on May 16 at the age of fifty-three.

Despite his young age, Jim had written letters to his five children to be opened only after his death. He insisted that at his funeral no one was to wear black and that it should be open to the public. More than five thousand people in bright colors filled the Cathedral of St. John the Divine in New York. At the door, Muppeteers distributed to the mourners two thousand foam butterflies suspended on rods, and when Harry Belafonte sang "Turn the World Around," the air inside the cathedral was swarmed with whirling butterflies. Finally, Carroll Spinny dressed as Big Bird came forward to sing the theme song Jim Henson had sung as Kermit, "It's Not Easy Being Green." Several times his voice broke, but at the end, looking up toward heaven, Big Bird said, "Thank you, Kermit." Then he bowed and slowly walked away.

Points to Ponder

1. Have you ever wondered (or even noticed) that most young boys' games are lengthened by arguments over the rules (which the boys seem to enjoy at least as much as the game itself), while quite often girls will change the rules—or even the game itself—for those who are unskilled? Maybe boys and girls react differently to games (and one another) because of their gender—the objective *nature* of their eventual different roles in family—but the differences are surely intensified by their *nurture*, their upbringing. Do you think that boys are more assertive and girls more sensitive

because of the different ways they are raised and the different ways that they play?

2. Most children can get along at play with a few crayons and a couple of empty cartons. These can magically change into chariots or castles. Recently, more and more "fortunate" children have intricate toys that do a great deal of the imagining *for* them. Television and video games contribute to this deficiency. And somewhere around the end of first grade (it seems), even schooling stops being so intriguing and gets down to the "serious business" of preparing for the SATs and job-searching! What are some ways that children (and adults) can retrieve the use of their imaginations?

3. Jim Henson said that "the most sophisticated people I know—inside, they're all children." Think of the adults you know. Do you think Jim Henson's words are really true? Do you have any evidence to suggest that inside even the worst Ebenezer Scrooges you know there are really Peter Pans struggling against years and years of layered disappointments to escape and be free?

seven

• • • • • •

Eleanor Roosevelt

• • • • • • • • • • • • • • • • • • •

First Lady of the United States

1884–1962

Empathy:

Pronunciation: \em-pə-thē\
Function: *noun*
Etymology: Greek *empatheia*, literally, passion, from
empathēs emotional, from *em-* + *pathos* feelings, emotion
Date: 1850
1: the imaginative projection of a subjective state into an
object so that the object appears to be infused with it
2: the action of understanding, being aware of,
being sensitive to, and vicariously experiencing the
feelings, thoughts, and experience of another of
either the past or present without having the feelings,
thoughts, and experience fully communicated in an
objectively explicit manner; *also:* the capacity for this

◇◇◇

*If you just learn a single trick, Scout, you'll get along a lot
better with all kinds of folks. You never really understand
a person until you consider things from his point of view,
until you climb inside of his skin and walk around in it.*
                          —Atticus Finch, from Harper Lee's
                                       To Kill a Mockingbird

◇◇◇

*Then the righteous will answer him and say, "Lord, when did
we see you hungry and feed you, or thirsty and give you drink?
When did we see you a stranger and welcome you, or naked
and clothe you? When did we see you ill or in prison, and visit
you?" And the king will say to them in reply, "Amen, I say
to you, whatever you did for one of these least brothers of
mine, you did for me."*
                                          —Matthew 25:37–40

Picture a shy little girl with lovely, sad eyes and
with slight bucked teeth protruding from pudding
cheeks. To have called the girl homely might have
been mean, but nevertheless thought and perhaps spoken
by others. And she was so solemn and painfully shy that
her own mother poked fun at her, calling her "Granny."
The parents of this child were among the most glamorous
couples in New York in the prosperous 1890s. Eleanor
Roosevelt's young parents, Elliott and Anna, were the
toast of the city's social life, their glamour overpowering
to the little girl who was like a mockingbird misplaced
among nightingales. Though she adored her charming,
irresponsible, often drunk father, little Eleanor hardly ever

saw her popular parents; she was tended by servants, which made her even more withdrawn.

When she was eight, her mother gave birth to a boy, Elliott, Jr., and a year later another brother, Hall was born. Finally at her wit's end with her husband's alcoholism, Anna Roosevelt insisted he be hospitalized and separated from the family for a year until he could sober up. Eleanor longed for her father and resented her mother for keeping them apart, yet when Anna was bedridden for days with excruciating headaches, the little girl sat for hours by her bed, massaging her mother's aching temples. "Feeling that I was useful was perhaps the greatest joy I experienced," she recalled years later.

Anna Roosevelt caught diphtheria and died in December 1892. A girl of ten, Eleanor grieved her mother's passing but couldn't contain the joy that her beloved father would be coming home. Yet even after her death, Anna prevented that; her will stipulated that the three children be granted to Anna's stern mother, Mary Ludlow Hall. Eleanor felt more alienated than ever. Within a year of her mother's death, her brother Elliott succumbed to scarlet fever. Her beloved father also tragically died from a fatal fall during a drinking bout. Eleanor later reflected that all the tragedies she endured as a lonely child evoked in her a profound sense of kinship with all lonely, deprived, and excluded children. This kinship would form the fabric for much of her life's work.

Eleanor submerged herself in her books, which did not enhance her attractiveness as she moved into her teens. Her severe grandmother dressed her in shapeless dresses that did nothing to improve her now gangling figure. One of her escapes, besides reading, was her visits to her uncle Teddy Roosevelt's rough-and-tumble family with all the kinds of child's play that went on there, but those moments of real family life were few.

Finally, a door opened to Eleanor when her grandmother sent her to Allenswood, a girls' boarding school
outside of London. There, Marie Souvestre, the head-
mistress, took a special interest in this overly reserved
girl. In February 1901, she took Eleanor on a trip to France
and Italy; she found the new places "a revelation." Eleanor
was so exhilarated by Allenswood that she wanted to
return for a fourth year, but Grandmother Hall adamantly
refused, insisting she return to make her official debut in
New York society—an event she dreaded. At eighteen she
was still taller than nearly any boy she was supposed to
dance with, and she was helpless at the chitchat expected
of young girls, preferring to talk politics, which withered
her chances even further. "I didn't quite realize beforehand
what utter agony it would be."

Another relative who seemed to offer her hope was her
father's sister, Anna Roosevelt Cowles. During visits to
her home in Washington, D.C., Eleanor found all sorts of
interesting, well-read, concerned people like herself, and
not least of these was Mrs. Cowles' brother and Eleanor's
uncle, President Teddy Roosevelt. Eleanor saw how much
the President valued her aunt's advice on affairs of state,
and she saw a woman could in fact affect national affairs,
not only among the affluent but also with the obscure
people with whom she felt such a pained kinship. Eleanor
soon after joined the Junior League, a group of wealthy
young woman working for the poor in hospitals and
settlement houses. Working in the slums of New York, she
found the squalor and want not daunting, but challeng-
ing. Indignant at the sordid conditions, low wages, and
long hours in the sweatshops—even for children of four
or five—Eleanor made it her task to visit businesses and
report to the Consumers' League about their inhuman
practices. "I was frightened to death," she wrote later, "but
I wanted to be useful."

Meanwhile, in the far more daunting round of parties, teas, and dances, she renewed a lifelong acquaintance with a distant cousin, the dashing and intellectual Franklin Roosevelt, who was finishing at Harvard and seemed to value aspects of Eleanor that shallower minds had ignored. In December 1903, he proposed that they marry. She was astonished, as was Franklin's domineering mother, Sara, who prevailed upon her only child to delay the engagement a year, hoping for someone better. But the following year, when Franklin entered Columbia Law School, they announced their engagement. In March 1905, they were married, with President Theodore Roosevelt giving away the bride. The couple spent the summer honeymooning in Europe.

When the couple returned to New York, Eleanor was happily pregnant, but her joy deflated when she found her mother-in-law had rented and furnished them an apartment, complete with hand-picked servants, only two blocks from her own home. The Roosevelts' first child, Anna, was born in May of 1906. To Eleanor, she was "just a helpless bundle, but by its mere helplessness winding itself inextricably around my heart." Precariously, she began to trust and love. In ten years, she gave birth to five more children, four of whom survived. The family spent the year in New York and summers on Campobello Island in Canada.

But it was not ideal. Responsibility for the children frightened Eleanor, unsure she could ever really do what was best for them. Worse, Sara Roosevelt built them a home in Hyde Park that was connected to her own so that she could walk in at any time, day or night. Her dictatorial nature more or less "took over" the children. Trapped between such an unflinching mother-in-law and such an ambitious husband, Eleanor became more and more withdrawn and inaccessible.

In 1910, Franklin was elected to the New York state legislature, and the family had to move to Albany and away from Franklin's mother, thankfully. Three years later, he was appointed assistant secretary of the Navy, and they moved to Washington, D.C. Dutifully, Eleanor realized the wife of an up-and-coming politician could no longer sit in the parlor reading. She began socializing, visiting the wives of other politicians and cementing new relationships. When World War I began, Eleanor joined the Navy Relief Society and served meals to soldiers passing through Washington's Union Station. For the Red Cross she visited hospitals, where she campaigned for further funding to care for battle-scarred veterans. Eleanor began to believe that she could make a difference, not only as a support for her husband but as an individual woman.

When her husband ran as vice president on the Democratic ticket in 1920, Eleanor campaigned vigorously not only for the Democrats, but for women to exercise their newly won right to vote. When the ticket was defeated, the Roosevelts returned to New York, and Franklin took up law practice. Then, while the family was on vacation at Campobello, Franklin fell victim to polio.

The couple's will was unyielding. Franklin resolved he would one day walk again, and he did (though only with the help of heavy iron leg braces), and Eleanor pledged that she would take his place until he could be active again. She threw herself into Democratic politics, leaving behind her aristocratic background and taking up the cause of those in society who seemed to have no voices or chances. She joined the Women's Trade Union League and organized women to campaign for a forty-hour work week, the abolition of child labor, and a minimum wage. She campaigned for Al Smith for president in 1928 and for her husband when he became well enough to run successfully for governor of New York. Then in 1932, in the midst of the Depression, Eleanor helped Franklin D.

Roosevelt win the election as the thirty-second President of the United States. Suddenly, the little goose had become a queen, but her story would not end like the storybooks.

In the White House, Eleanor moved heavy furniture, operated the elevator for herself, and invited anyone who chose—white or black, rich or poor—to tour the house for which their taxes paid the rent. Eleanor allowed only female reporters at her press conferences, and she began a monthly column in *Women's Home Companion*, inviting anyone in the country to write to her about their concerns. In her first year as First Lady, three hundred thousand responded. She began giving radio talks and lectures. Asked if her husband's illness had affected his mind, she answered unflappably, "Anyone who has gone through suffering is bound to have greater sympathy and understanding." She herself proved that.

Eleanor Roosevelt's work on behalf of African Americans preceded the civil rights movement by three decades. She invited blacks—from sharecroppers to black-college presidents—to the White House to offer a forum for them to communicate their frustrations with slow-moving social change to the government. Invited to a meeting in Alabama where it was illegal for her to sit with her black friends, she set her chair in the middle aisle between the black and white sides. In 1939, when the Daughters of the American Revolution denied Constitution Hall to black singer Marian Anderson, Eleanor resigned her membership and worked behind the scenes for a free concert in front of the Lincoln Memorial, which seventy-five thousand people attended.

As World War II began, Franklin was elected to an unprecedented third term, due largely to Eleanor's speech at the Democratic National Convention, calming explosive factions and urging unity. Although the United States had resolved to remain neutral, the Japanese attack on Pearl Harbor, December 7, 1941, rendered that impossible.

While President Roosevelt made a diplomatic tour of free Europe, Eleanor made a tour to servicemen in the South Pacific. The commander, Admiral William "Bull" Halsey was none too pleased at first, but quickly changed his mind when he saw that this woman was not merely paying a quick photo-opportunity courtesy call to each hospital. She went to every ward, every bed, meeting every wounded man personally. Eleanor had four sons in service herself, and for those boys she visited, her presence was almost like a visit from their own mothers.

As the war began drawing to a painful close, and only eighty-two days into his fourth term as president, Franklin Roosevelt died in Warm Springs, Georgia. He had been wearied well beyond his sixty-three years. When the new president, Harry Truman, came to see Eleanor at the White House, he asked if there was anything he could do for her, but she said, "Is there anything I can do for *you*?"

When the war ended four months later, Truman took her at her word, appointing her a delegate to the newly forming United Nations, where she headed the commission drafting a Universal Declaration of Human Rights. She also worked for the million refugees in internment camps all over Europe, many of which she visited. Truman also used her as a goodwill ambassador to Lebanon, Pakistan, India, and the newly emergent Third World, where thousands of people greeted her at each stop. Typically, she thought they had shown up out of respect for her late husband, not out of respect for her. When she spoke at the 1952 Democratic Convention, the chairman called for order: "Will the delegates please take their seats? Several million people are waiting to hear the First Lady of the World."

When President Eisenhower accepted her resignation from the United Nation's post when she was seventy-three, Eleanor agreed to an invitation from the *New York Post* to travel as a correspondent to the Soviet Union, during which time she had a two-and-a-half-hour interview with Soviet President Nikita Khrushchev, after which he said, "At least we didn't shoot one another." But she added, "Either all of us are going to die together, or we are going to learn to live together, and if we are to live together we have to talk."

On November 7, 1962, Eleanor Roosevelt died in New York City. As she had told reporters on her seventy-seventh birthday, "Life was meant to be lived. Curiosity must be kept alive. The fatal thing is the rejection of it. One must never, for whatever reason, turn his back on life."

Points to Ponder

1. We've all known people who have suffered profoundly—long physical agony, family abuse, temptations to disillusionment or even despair. Each victim freely chooses—or at least submits to—an *attitude* toward not only the suffering itself but also to the value of life. Some become embittered and whiny; others become belligerent and vengeful. But still others—like most people in these pages—have a totally different, almost contradictory reaction to difficult challenges. What rescued them? What people and practices kept their heads resolutely above the quicksand and helped them triumph over their pain?

2. Another reaction to consistent setbacks in childhood and adolescence is an independence that stands up to challenge, refusing to be broken in spirit. But in some, that self-reliance can be impoverishing, acting on the conviction that "I can do it *alone*!" What happens to people who refuse to be helped? What happens to people who refuse to let themselves be *loved*?

3. The philosopher Aristotle said that we learn to be confident by acting confident—even though we don't at all feel it the

first several times we try. Far too many people back away from having a personally validated self by copping out. "Oh, I was raised to be more reserved," or, "I just stand up and tell them where they can go!" They blame their bad habits on their personalities rather than blaming themselves for both. Everybody has a personality, that is, a cluster of habits we developed (without the ability to think) in instinctive response to parents, siblings, and the environment. Some end up assertive, some withdrawn. But when we arrived at adolescence, we had a chance to take charge of that personality and to recognize its assets and develop them and to accept its liabilities and begin to uproot those bad habits. Where is your starting point to be your best you?

eight

• • • • • •

Lech Walesa

• • • • • • • • • • • •

Union Organizer, Politician, Activist

1943–

Passion:

Pronunciation: \pa-shən\
Function: *noun*
Etymology: Middle English, from Anglo-French, from
Late Latin *passion-*, *passio* suffering, being acted upon,
from Latin *pati* to suffer
Date: 13th century
1a: Emotion **b:** intense, driving, overmastering feeling or
conviction

◇◇◇

We all need to look into the dark side of our nature—that's
where the energy is, the passion. People are afraid of
that because it holds pieces of us we're busy denying.
—Sue Grafton

◇◇◇

*"I know your works; I know that you are neither cold nor hot. I
wish you were either cold or hot. So, because you are lukewarm,
neither hot nor cold, I will spit you out of my mouth."*
                                                    —Revelation 3:15–16

I n the early evening of Thursday, November 9, 1989, the
twelve-foot-high Berlin Wall, which for twenty-eight
years had stretched ninety-seven miles between the
Soviet and the Allied sectors of the former German capital,
began very slowly to disintegrate—because of a simple
mistake.

For months, the Soviet-dominated countries of Eastern
Europe had been boiling with unrest. Frustrated crowds
by the thousands were demonstrating in Czechoslovakia,
Hungary, Poland, and East Germany because of policies
strangling human freedoms and punishing prices for food
and basic consumer goods. That day, Günter Schabowski,
the East German Minister of Propaganda, had received
orders from the Politburo, the ruling communist political
party, to announce that (in order to prevent a large-scale
riot) border crossings between the two sectors would be
somewhat eased. Dutifully, he gave the announcement to
reporters with no specifics, since he had none. But when
that vague declaration became public, thousands upon
thousands of Berliners showed up on both sides of all the
checkpoints between the sectors so that the overwhelmed
border guards had no choice but to get out of their way!

By nightfall, hundreds of young people from both
sides had shinnied up to the top of the wall, looking across
the 100-yard "death strip" where 196 East Germans had
been killed trying to escape to West Berlin since 1961.

They began to chip away with pickaxes, like small chinks in an immense dike. In less than a month, the Wall had crumbled, and with it came the collapse of European communism.

Several world figures have been credited with that thunderous victory: American president Ronald Reagan, Soviet premier Mikhail Gorbachev, and the Polish pope John Paul II, but no single individual could have breached that wall or the Iron Curtain it embodied unless thousands of "nobodies" had taken heart and stood up, refusing to be dehumanized any longer. One of the most notable of those "small people" who ignited confidence in others was a foxy, ginger-haired, mustachioed Polish electrician, armed with no more than a vocational-school education and his own indomitable passion. His name was Lech Walesa (pronounced vow-EN-sa).

Lech Walesa was the son of a carpenter. His father had been conscripted by the Russians to dig ditches before he died of hunger and ill treatment when Lech was only three years old. After vocational school, Lech worked for four years as a car mechanic before securing a better job in 1967 as an electrician in the Lenin Shipyards of Gdansk (formerly Danzig), the city where the Second World War began.

The cost of living was nearly unbearable. Price subsidies to farmers began absorbing a staggering one-third of the national budget so that farmers bought bread to feed their livestock because it was cheaper than the wheat it was made from. In 1970, the workers' displeasure with oppression erupted in a bloody strike in which forty-four people were killed and a thousand injured by the riot police. As a member of the strike committee, Lech was arrested and imprisoned for nearly a year. Even when he was released, because he was on a blacklist for "antisocial behavior," he was refused a job, and he and his new wife, Danuta, had to depend on relatives and friends to survive.

It was in the mid-1970s that the Catholic Church, which represented by far the majority of Poles, began to speak out more strongly against the communist regime. Then in 1979, its voice thundered around the world when Pope John Paul II, the former archbishop of Krakow as Karol Wojtyla and now the first Polish pope, visited Poland and was cheered wildly by millions of Poles in each place he went. Pope John Paul II never said an actionable word against the regime, but the strength of his position and personality was an incalculable boost to the forces of resistance.

By July 1980 skyrocketing food prices and the imposition of wage controls sparked another round of protests and strikes along the Baltic coast, and workers occupied their factories and refused to work or budge. But just as their resolve was beginning to wear dangerously thin, Lech Walesa emerged again, climbing over the factory wall and hollering at them to begin the strike. Lech's blue-collar Polish was rough and often ungrammatical, and years of heavy smoking made his voice rasp like an iron file, but his irresistible gift was the passion of his conviction and his talent for distilling complex issues into simple words and images everyone could understand. In no time, he was chosen to chair the strikers' committee.

Lech had a game plan for the strike. Like soldiers before battle, the strikers confessed their sins, celebrated Mass, and received Communion from a group of equally daring Catholic priests in the open shipyard. In order to deter violence, Lech called for a ban on alcohol and demanded strict discipline. Through it all, his spunk and infectious humor helped the workers gain a sense of the power that came from their fellowship.

Three days after the strike began, the government buckled, but the workers forged ahead seeking more gains, and they were joined by half a million others who demanded the right to form a union to represent them with government-controlled industries across Poland. Ironically, the right to form a union was a condition that the communist regime had been promising Poles for thirty-five years.

Ten million workers and farmers, a quarter of the population, joined into a national federation of unions named *Solidarnosc* (Solidarity), with Lech Walesa at its head. But for all his zeal, Lech was not a hot-headed zealot. Much to the concern of his more impulsive co-unionists, he kept insisting on cooperation with the government and only cautious and gradual introduction of reform, lest they antagonize the sullen bear of the Soviet Union, which could at any time send in their tanks, as they had in Hungary in 1956.

The exhilaration of freedom was contagious. Government easement of censorship brought an outpouring of critical newspaper articles, books, films, and television. The government did respond to these protests. In December, 1981, the new prime minister, Wojciech Jaruzelski, imposed martial law, in violation of even the communist constitution, and warned of the imminent Soviet invasion. Polish tanks clanked across the country. Soldiers and police put down any worker resistance. Universities closed. Solidarity was outlawed, and thousands were arrested. Lech was rousted from bed at 3:00 a.m. and imprisoned in a government "guesthouse" south of Warsaw for nearly a year.

When he was released from prison, Lech applied for his old job back at the shipyard and became, for a while, a simple electrician again, although he was under virtual house arrest. But Lech's life was not destined to remain simple for much longer.

In 1983, to the worldwide embarrassment of the Polish government, Lech Walesa was awarded the Nobel Peace Prize. Rightly fearing that, if he were to go to Oslo, Norway, to accept the award, the government would bar his return, his wife accepted the prize in his place. He donated the award of over a million dollars to the Solidarity Committee in exile in Brussels. The Nobel Committee citation read:

> Lech Walesa's contribution is more than a domestic Polish concern; the solidarity for which he is spokesman is an expression of precisely the concept of being at one with humanity; therefore he belongs to us all. . . . The presentation of the Peace Prize to him today is an homage to the power which abides in one person's belief, in his vision and in his courage to follow his call.

In 1985, Mikhail Gorbachev, a practical man rather than an ideologue, became the leader of the Soviet Union. Gorbachev initiated the policies of *glasnost* (open discussion) and *perestroika* (restructuring). Because of continued Polish unrest, General Jaruzelski was forced to reach out to the still-outlawed, but very powerful, Solidarity and its leader, Lech Walesa, who had convinced the other noncommunist parties to join in a united front. After ninety-four roundtable sessions over two months, the Party was forced to agree to the first elected Polish legislature—even though it demanded assurance that 65 percent of the seats would go to communists. In the election, however, Solidarity won ninety-nine of the one hundred seats allotted to non-communists. When Jaruzelski tried to persuade the elected Solidarity members to join the communists in a "grand coalition," Lech refused, saying that Solidarity's goal was to liberate Poland from communist-Soviet oppression.

After Solidarity's goal was reached and Poland was finally liberated from the Soviet Union, Lech was elected Polish president in 1990. He served as president for five years before losing reelection by only one percent of the claimed he possessed a university degree and used Lech's lack of higher education as a political weapon. To be honest, some found him "too undignified to be a head of state." For instance, when he stayed as a guest of Queen Elizabeth at Windsor Castle, he joked, "The bed was so big, I couldn't find my wife."

Lech Walesa was like unrefined gold to Poland and the Solidarity movement. He remains an undiplomatic, pigheaded, and yet completely human man. His humor and passion ignited the slumbering soul of the Polish people in the 1970s and '80s, and his abrasiveness wore away what seemed an impenetrable communist slave system.

"I built a democracy," he said, "and then I turned it over to democracy."

Points to Ponder

1. In our culture, the word "passion" has become almost exclusively limited to sexuality. Lech Walesa's passion was another kind entirely—the kind of ardor that made Joan of Arc ride relentlessly into battle, Galileo spend night after night at his telescope, Christy Nolan and Helen Keller battle to *escape* the prisons of their bodies. As the Nobel Committee wrote of Lech Walesa, "[He has] the power which abides in one person's belief." Where does that kind of passion really come from? What is life like when people don't live with that kind of fervor?

2. Our culture also seems to have a love/hate relationship with the rough-hewn and down-and-dirty characters like Indiana Jones, Erin Brockovich, and Lara Croft. On the one hand, personnel managers (who are the gatekeepers to "a decent job") hire men and women who are "proper," deodorized, mannerly, predictable—in a word, "domesticated." Yet people have something thwarted inside that wants to shed the neckties and heels, the aftershave and curlers, and grab

hold of the type of freedom rock stars seem to enjoy and flaunt with their ripped shirts, jeans, and unkempt hair. That force is what Freud called the *id*, the wolf in each of us, left behind in us from our animal forebears. You can suppress it, but it won't go away. In the story "The Three Little Pigs," the wise third pig didn't kill the wolf and bury him; he ate the wolf—made it a vibrant, controlled part of himself. How does someone control that primal power in each of us, use it in service of our life goals?

3. For centuries, religious groups have written stories of their denomination's heroes called "Lives of the Saints." In most cases, the people celebrated in them were genuinely loving, selfless, and brave, but almost inevitably the writers went off the deep end, making their subjects plaster saints— antiseptically faultless, often to the point of absurdity, so that they were not only beyond imitation but actually repellant to anyone with half a mind. Can someone be a good and genuine model of human behavior and still have character defects? If not, how is aspiring to be a genuine human being a futile endeavor?

nine

· · · · ·

Clara Hale

· · · · · · · · · · ·

Humanitarian, Foster Parent

1905–1992

Kindness:

Pronunciation: \kīn(d)-nəs\
Function: *noun*
Date: 13th century
1: a kind deed: favor
2 a: the quality or state of being kind. **b:** archaic: affection

◇◇◇

*Constant kindness can accomplish much. As the sun
makes ice melt, kindness causes misunderstanding,
mistrust, and hostility to evaporate.*
—Albert Schweitzer

◇◇◇

*He who does a kindness is remembered afterward; when he falls,
he finds a support.*
—Sirach 4:30

Every year, approximately five thousand infants are born in the United States to mothers addicted to heroin, methadone, cocaine, and other hard drugs, more than half of them in metropolitan New York City alone. Through no choice of their own, these babies are born with a craving for narcotics from the very first instant they breathe. Whether the mother seeks treatment or not, the infant goes through the same agony of withdrawal as a long-time drug addict: twisting in torment and enduring terrifying images while also suffering from weeks of diarrhea, vomiting, and red-faced screaming while inflicting bloody scratches on their bodies because of their need for drugs.

In the twenty-four years between 1969 and her death at age eighty-seven in 1993, Clara Hale cared for more than five hundred of these babies as a foster mother. Everyone who knew her called her "Mother Hale." And rightly so.

In 1923, after graduation from high school, Clara Hale and her husband, Thomas, moved from Philadelphia to Harlem. He ran a floor-waxing business; she cleaned movie theaters after the last show so she could spend the days with their children: Lorraine, Nathan, and Kenneth. Clara had been no stranger to hard work or bad breaks. Her father was murdered when she was an infant, and her mother supported the family by taking in boarders and cooking for longshoremen. Clara said that her mother gave her "the foundation of all I've done: to love people, to be proud of myself, and always to look people in the eyes."

Thomas died of cancer in 1932 when Clara was only twenty-seven, leaving her with little money and three children under six. For several years, she supplemented her theater-cleaning income by cleaning people's apartments during the day. But reluctant to leave her own youngsters, she started babysitting working mothers' children for $2 a week each, then keeping children the whole week for mothers who were live-in maids. Clara eventually became a licensed foster mother.

For the next twenty-seven years, her five-room walk-up apartment on West 146th Street was home for seven or eight foster children at a time. "I didn't make a whole lot," she said, "but I wasn't starving. And the kids must've liked it because once they got there, they didn't want to go home. My daughter says she was almost sixteen before she realized those other kids weren't her real sisters and brothers. I took care of forty of them like that. They're now all grown up. Doctors, lawyers, everything. Almost all of them stay in touch. And now I have about sixty 'grandchildren.'"

In 1968, at the age of sixty-three, Clara Hale thought it was time for her to "just kinda take it easy." But a year later, her daughter, Lorraine, who had attained a doctorate in child development, was driving along 146th Street and noticed a drug-addicted woman sitting on a crate, nodding stuporously with her two-month-old baby about to slip out of her arms. Impulsively, Lorraine stopped, jumped out of the car, roused the woman, and gave her Clara's address as a place "where you can get your baby help." Next morning, Clara called Lorraine and said, "There's a junkie at my door, and she says you sent her." And so she became "Mother" Hale. She took the baby, and soon a steady stream of addicted babies found their way to her door. "Before I knew it, every pregnant addict in Harlem knew about the crazy lady who would give her baby a home."

Within two months, she was caring for twenty-two addicted babies, packed wall-to-wall in cribs in her five-room apartment. Working at two jobs each, Mother Hale's three children provided the sole financial support for a year and a half, until Percy Sutton, then Manhattan Borough President, persuaded the city, state, and federal governments to undertake the costs. Funds came from individuals such as Lena Horne and Tony Bennett. John Lennon gave Mother Hale $30,000, and his widow, Yoko Ono, continued to send her $20,000 annually after Lennon's murder in 1980.

The treatment was hardly complicated. "We hold them and touch them. They love you to tell them how great they are, how good they are. Somehow, even at that young age, they understand that." Until the week she died, Mother Hale awoke each morning to give 6:00 a.m. bottles to addicted infants who shared her room. She cleaned up their vomit, changed their diapers, fed them lunch and dinner, and tried to nap when they did. When they cried out in the torment of withdrawal, she walked the floor with them, singing and talking. Mother Hale never gave medicine to the children, not even aspirin. "I don't want them to get in any habits; they go cold turkey." Instead, she cuddled, rocked, and cooed, knowing "one day they'll smile at me." Ninety-percent recovered, and if their mothers successfully completed drug rehabilitation, most returned to their moms, both now better after the excruciating experience.

Percy Sutton also began the search for a house that would suit Mother Hale's escalating needs and found a vacant five-story brownstone at 154 West 122nd Street, which was gutted and then rebuilt with a federal grant. It opened as Hale House in 1975, only six years after that first woman had showed up at Mother Hale's door. The first floor was a playroom for pre-school activities and also had a kitchen and dining room covered with mirrors. "I want my kids," she said, "when they pass by those mirrors to see themselves and say to themselves that they look nice." The second floor was set up as a nursery for detoxified babies, usually about ten days old, who stayed with Mother Hale in her third-floor bedroom during their period of withdrawal before moving downstairs.

After withdrawal had ended, when infants could sleep through the night, they moved from Mother Hale's bedroom to the floor below, where trained child-care workers watched over them. Older children shared rooms on the fourth floor. While undergoing rehab, usually for eighteen months, mothers were required to visit their babies regularly. The aim was to reunite mothers and children, and of the five hundred children who lived in Hale House during Mother Hale's life, only twelve were offered for adoption. Mother Hale stoutly maintained all her life, "This is not an orphanage."

Hale House eventually expanded to include housing and education for mothers after detox, apprentice training for children beginning to get into trouble, and a home for mothers and infants infected with AIDS. Those born with AIDS faced a drastically shortened life of suffering, which Mother Hale and her helpers vowed to make as easeful as they could make it.

Her daughter Lorraine eventually took over administration of Hale House, leaving her mother free to deal directly with the children. There were several child-care workers and three sleep-in aides to help Mother Hale in her job, which was, she said, "just to love the children." Other staff positions included a house parent, a social worker, a teacher, a cook, and a maintenance worker. A part-time health staff provided medical and dental care along with a local clinic. At the beginning, the staff worked for about $175 a week.

Mother Hale's generosity was not limited to children. Lorraine told a reporter, "Anybody can come to my mother for a handout, and she'll give it. She gets paid a salary, and she gives it all away. We finally got her to open a checking account at the age of seventy-six. Every month, I write thirty envelopes to different causes she supports."

President Ronald Reagan invited Mother Hale to attend his State of the Union address February 6, 1985.

"When the President called, I was sick, but I went anyway. I wanted the kids to know it. The doctor said I shouldn't, because I might have a stroke, but I told him, when the President calls, I go." She sat in the visitors' gallery of the House of Representatives, and when Reagan looked up and hailed her as "an angel . . . a true American hero," everyone present—senators, representatives, the Supreme Court, and the cabinet—rose to their feet in a standing ovation.

"Everyone comes into this world to do something, and I found what I was meant to do. I love children, and I love caring for them," she said. "I'm not an American hero. I'm simply a person who loves children."

Empathy makes the heart reach out. Kindness goes for the hands.

Points to Ponder

1. "They love you to tell them how great they are, how good they are." Out of a deadly false humility, many of us say, "Oh, I'm nobody." Tragically, that becomes a self-fulfilling prophecy: If you act like a nobody, you'll *be* a nobody, and few will mourn your passing. Surely there's at least one other "nobody" whom you encounter between the time you wake and the time you sleep—the one who rarely, if ever, smiles and who scuttles away at the least threat of intrusion. What *might* happen if you put out your hand and said, "Hi!" and told that person your name? Your life will make little difference if you don't believe you have something to give and have the confidence to offer it.

2. There's a vast difference—and distance—between pity and kindness. It's true that you simply can't reach out to every needful cause, but you certainly could choose just one worthy cause and do for it what you *can*. What prevents you?

3. There was once an otherwise nondescript television com-
mercial in which an uninterested passerby notices some
one else stepping out to pull back someone about to be
splashed by a passing car. A minute later that same person
sees a woman with a baby who's dropped her groceries and
stops to pick them up with her. And on and on. Kindness
can be contagious. Do you suspect you yourself could set in
motion that kind of "plague" of thoughtfulness?

ten

• • •

Will Rogers

• • • • • • • • • • • •

Humorist, Social Commentator, Cowboy

1879–1935

Honesty:

Pronunciation: \ä-nəs-tē\
Function: *noun*
Date: 14th century
1 *obsolete:* chastity
2 a: fairness and straightforwardness of conduct
b: adherence to the facts: sincerity

◇◇◇

*A man who lies to himself, and believes his own lies, becomes
unable to recognize truth, either in himself or in anyone else,
and he ends up losing respect for himself and for others. When
he has no respect for anyone, he can no longer love, and in
him, he yields to his impulses, indulges in the lowest form of
pleasure, and behaves in the end like an animal in satisfying
his vices. And it all comes from lying to others and to yourself.*
—Fyodor Dostoevsky

◇◇◇

Make no mistake: God is not mocked, for a person will reap only what he sows.

—Galatians 6:7

Will Rogers was a quarter-blood Cherokee Indian, whose ancestors had trekked in the winter of 1838 along the so-called "Trail of Tears," when the government forced Cherokees from their ancestral home in Georgia to the Indian Territory near the border of Arkansas and Oklahoma. After service in the Confederate Army, Will's father, Clem, settled his family on a homestead on the banks of the Verdigris River, three miles east of the town of Oologah, Oklahoma. The last of eight children, Will learned to ride horses as soon as he could walk, along with all the skills of a cowpuncher—breaking horses, roping, branding cattle, mending fences—but he didn't absorb much "book learning." In ten years at six schools, he estimated he probably got as far as fourth grade. Later in life, after he became a world-famous Vaudeville star, newspaper writer, journalist, adviser and representative of presidents, lecturer, and film star, Will understood that a diploma might be reassuring, but no substitute for discipline, drive, determination, and a dream.

Rodeos fascinated Will Rogers early on: bulldogging steers, riding wild horses, and doing fancy tricks with a lariat (which he became as skilled at as he was at dodging school). Like the Indian territory itself, the rodeo was a place that had no patience with sham or pretense; a man was judged by his skill and reliability. But cowboys were also known for wanderlust. At age eighteen, Will surrendered to his itchy feet, running away from military school, first to a ranch in Texas, then to San Francisco, and next to New York City. A few years later, he and a cowboy friend set out for Argentina, working ranches for no more than room and board. When a cattle buyer offered a job on a cattle boat headed for South Africa, Will jumped at the chance. He spent his time breaking broncos for British soldiers who he remembered "had about as much chance of staying on top of some of those renegades as a man would sneezing into a cyclone."

In December 1902, Will joined Texas Jack's Wild West Show as a trick rider and roper in Johannesburg. The following year he went with the Wirth Brothers Circus through Australia and New Zealand and finally returned to the States to join Colonel Zack Mulhall's Wild West Show at the St. Louis Exposition in 1904, then on to Madison Square Garden in New York City. There Will made his big decision: He wanted to go into Vaudeville.

Vaudeville was a popular form of stage entertainment in the United States from the late 1800s until around 1930. The variety shows featured singers, dancers, comedians, jugglers, magicians, acrobats, and Will figured his roping would be a unique addition. Unfortunately, his act proved too unique. He tramped from one agency to another, until finally he got a tryout at Keith's Union Theater in June 1905, where, without saying a word, he auditioned with a fancy rope trick called the "crinoline." In that trick Will began whirling the rope in a small circle overhead, gradually widening it and widening it until he circled far out into the audience. For a finale, a horse and rider suddenly erupted onto the stage, and Will threw two ropes, lassoing both the horse and the rider!

During all of Will's rope tricks he would also talk to himself as if oblivious of the audience. He'd say things like, "Swinging a rope is all right when your neck ain't in it. Then it's hell." His casual, drawled humor began to catch on, and within a year he was traveling with a show through Europe. Around this time, in 1902, Will married Betty Blake, a woman he had fallen in love with before his time in South America. Betty married him despite her hesitation about the vagabond life of Vaudeville. And after the birth of their first two children, Will, Jr., and Mary Amelia, Betty persuaded Will to buy a house in Amityville, New York, where he could be near the city but where the children could have a less hectic life.

In 1916, impresario Florenz Ziegfeld hired Will to perform at his nightclub. The regular job was good, except that since many of the audience came back night after night, Will was strapped to keep his comic material fresh. His wife suggested he get ideas from the newspapers. Suddenly the comic had become a humorist, commenting on daily events. Will broke into the big time when he was hired in the *Ziegfeld Follies*, a Broadway production. By that time he was concentrating less on the roping and more on the homespun humor, seeing how his audiences warmed to the truth—spiced with a bit of exaggeration. The *New York Times* described his act: "He begins talking in his Oklahoma drawl, and all the while chewing gum and playing with the ropes. When he begins to make the ropes writhe like snakes and strike the bull's-eye time and again with his quaint homely wit, you are as proud of him as if you had done it yourself."

A turning point in Will's style and confidence came when he played before President Woodrow Wilson at the Friars' Club Frolic in Baltimore. He had always poked fun at politicians, but when he began fooling around about Wilson's sending General Pershing into Mexico to apprehend the bandit Pancho Villa, "everybody in the house looked at the President before they would laugh, to see how he was going to take it. Well, he started laughing, and they all followed suit." If you can poke fun at the president and get away with it, anything else is fair game.

On the last day of 1922, the *Times* wrote, "The famous cowboy monologist, Will Rogers, has undertaken to write for this paper a weekly article of humorous comment upon contemporary affairs." Will's column became an instant hit and was syndicated in papers all over the world. His readers chuckled as he deflated the pompous and self-righteous politicians and businessmen. In 1926, The *Saturday Evening Post* sent him on a tour of Europe for a series of articles, which also became a book, *Letters of a Self-Made Diplomat to His President*. In 1932, he traveled throughout the Far East and eventually went around the world three times. Will also tried his hand at acting in films. By 1919, Will had appeared in several forgettable silent films, but in 1929, he began to appear in a string of talkies, most notably *A Connecticut Yankee in King Arthur's Court* and *Steamboat 'Round the Bend*. In 1926, he made his first radio broadcast, then signed a contract for a weekly show.

Will Rogers was in the tradition of the cracker-box philosophers, wise old codgers who sat in the local store on a cracker barrel and doled out wisdom. Like Artemus Ward, Josh Billings, Mr. Dooley, and Mark Twain, he assumed a posture of ignorance in order to prick pompous balloons. Nothing dishonest or hypocritical escaped his critical eye, and he became a symbol of the "common man," a person of horse sense who was never deceived by political duplicity or misled by fads or unsound causes. Of the devastating treaty imposed by the Allies on Germany after World War I (which eventually brought Hitler to power), Will said, "The terms of the Armistice read like a mortgage, but this Peace Treaty sounds like a foreclosure."

Will Rogers had several foils for his humor, some of which are detailed below:

Although Will didn't drink himself, he resented Prohibition, the government making people's personal choices equivalent to crimes like robbery or assault. He pictured a prohibitionist who "presents a Medal to himself because he's going to *meddle* in everybody's business but his own."

He never hesitated to tell the truth, and always did so with a twinkle in his eye. Addressing the International Bankers Association in 1922, he said:

> Loan sharks and interest hounds! I have addressed every form of organized graft in the U.S., excepting Congress. So it's naturally a pleasure for me to appear before the biggest. You are probably the most disgustingly rich audience I ever talked to, with the possible exception of the Bootleggers Union Local No. 1, combined with law enforcement officers.

Congress provided Will ample material:

> They are having what is called a Filibuster in the Senate. The name is just as silly as the thing itself. It means that a man can get up and talk for fifteen or twenty years at a time, then he is relieved by another, just to keep some bill from coming to a vote, no matter whether it is good or bad. . . . Why, if a distinguished foreigner was to be taken into the Senate and not told what the institution was, and heard a man ramble on, talking that had been going on for ten or twelve hours, he would probably say, "You have lovely quarters for your insane, but have you no warden to see they don't talk themselves to death?"

Having read about the decline and fall of Rome, Will was prepared to be impressed by the city itself. He wasn't. "The Colosseum," he wrote, "has been a grand old building, but they stole enough off it to build everything else in Rome. Between reading something and actually seeing it, you can never tell till you see it just how big a liar History is. I didn't know before I got there that Rome had Senators. Now I know why it declined."

Dishonesty and corruption attracted Will's satire. When the papers published the amounts of taxes the super-rich paid, which seemed pretty paltry compared to the way they lived, he wrote:

Don't feel discouraged if a lot of our well-known men were not as wealthy according to the taxes as you thought they ought to be. They are just as rich as you thought. This publication of amounts had nothing to do with their wealth. It was only a test of their honesty, and gives you practically no idea of their wealth at all.

Ironically, it was Will's restless curiosity that led to his death. He had always been a great proponent of airplanes and had barnstormed with General Billy Mitchell and Charles Lindbergh. With his friend Wiley Post, a pioneer of air travel just back from an around-the-world tour, Will set out to test the possibility of an air route from Alaska to Siberia that would avoid the dangers of a long flight over the Pacific. They were flying from Fairbanks to Point Barrow, the westernmost point on the American continent, but their plane never arrived. A lone Eskimo fisherman saw the crash and reported in broken English: "Mans with sore eye [Post wore an eye patch] start engine and go up. Engine spit, start, then stop. Start some more little. Then plane fall just so." With his hands he indicated a bank, a fall on the right wing, a nose dive into the water, a complete somersault. Then silence.

Points to Ponder

1. If all you want is money and fame, even a grade-school diploma isn't required: see Henry Ford, Thomas Edison, Mark Twain, and Abraham Lincoln. Nor do you need even a college diploma: see Jim Carrey, Julia Roberts, John Steinbeck, Ernest Hemingway, and Bill Gates. All it takes is discipline, drive, determination—and a dream—which even graduate schools don't teach. If you hope to be a "success," where do you plan on picking up those four essential qualities? It's true that formal schooling *can* help, but the *Almanac* shows that about 75 percent of those gainfully employed never finished college. What would have to be put *into* formal education in order for it to be of any advantage to you?

2. Humorists of all sorts—satirists like Voltaire and Jonathan Swift, stand-ups like Steve Martin and Chris Rock, political cartoonists—have a refined sense of hypocrisy and pretense. The Marx Brothers always had a snooty society matron handy to catch a cream pie in the face. Pick out at least one public figure who gives off a scent of phoniness. If you were to picture this person as a comical character, what would you say about him or her that would be funny but not unkind?

3. Another quality of fascinating people is "restless curiosity." Think of older people you know who spark your interest as being "perky." Do they seem to have an interest in almost anything, their minds and imaginations percolating like bubbles in a boiling pot? Why don't they tolerate being bored for too long? How would someone like you begin to develop that life-enhancing habit?

eleven

Bono

Musician, Activist

1960–

Justice:

Pronunciation: \jəs-təs\
Function: *noun*
Etymology: Middle English, from Anglo-French *justise*, from Latin *justitia*, from *justus*
Date: 12th century
1 a: the maintenance or administration of what is fair, especially by the impartial adjustment of conflicting claims or the assignment of merited rewards or punishments **b:** judge **c:** the administration of law; especially: the establishment or determination of rights according to the rules of law or equity
2 a: the quality of being just, impartial, or fair **b** (1): the principle or ideal of just dealing or right action (2): conformity to this principle or ideal: righteousness **c:** the quality of conforming to law
3: conformity to truth, fact, or reason: correctness

◇◇◇

Human progress is neither automatic nor inevitable.
. . . Every step toward the goal of justice requires
sacrifice, suffering, and struggle; the tireless exertions
and passionate concern of dedicated individuals.

—Martin Luther King, Jr.

◇◇◇

Only if you thoroughly reform your ways and your deeds; if each
of you deals justly with his neighbor . . . will I remain with you
in this place, in the land which I gave your fathers long ago and
forever.

—Jeremiah 7:5, 7

E ven heads of state jostle to have a photo op with
Bono—likely to improve their own images. U2, the
rock band he formed with three school friends in a
north Dublin high school, has sold more than 170 million
albums worldwide and won twenty-two Grammy Awards,
more than any other group, and their concert tours have
brought uncountable millions to their feet cheering. At least
in some part due to his publicized persistence champion-
ing for the forgiveness of unpayable international debts
owed by poor nations to rich nations, a 2004 World Bank
study found that in countries receiving debt relief, poverty
reduction initiatives suddenly doubled. Tanzania used
the savings to eliminate school fees, hire more teachers,
and build more schools. Burkina Faso drastically reduced
the cost of life-saving drugs and increased access to clean
water. Uganda more than doubled its school enrollment.

Born Paul David Hewson in 1960, Bono has risen to great heights beyond the world of the music-recording industry. He was granted honorary British knighthood and was named a Person of the Year by *Time* in 2005. He was a nominee for the Nobel Peace Prize in 2003, 2005, and 2006. He is the only person in history to have been nominated for an Academy Award, Golden Globe, Grammy, and Nobel Peace Prize. He and his wife and four children live in a gated estate in Killiney, Ireland, and share a villa in Eze in the south of France with U2 bandmate The Edge, as well as a penthouse on Central Park West in Manhattan.

Not bad for a guy who admits, "When we started out I was the guitar player, along with The Edge—except I couldn't play guitar. I still can't. I was such a lousy guitar player that one day they broke it to me that maybe I should sing instead. I had tried before, but I had no voice at all. I remember the day I found I could sing. I said, 'Oh, that's how you do it.'"

Bono's own father described him as "a bloody exasperating child," and he was both forgetful and contentious, which earned him the extreme nickname "Antichrist" from both family and friends. When he was only three years old, playing in their backyard garden, his parents saw their toddler lift honeybees off flowers on his fingertip, talk to them, then put them back without ever getting stung. Later in school, he excelled in history and art, and girls adored his sweet-talking charm.

In the fall of 1976, three students at Mount Temple Comprehensive High School (where Christy Nolan was also a student) responded to a bulletin-board note from Larry Mullen, a drummer, to form a rock band. Paul Hewson responded to the ad along with David Evans and Adam Clayton. Paul's nickname "Bono" came from the misreading of the name of a local hearing-aid shop name, *Bonavox*, which means "good voice." Instead a mate tagged it onto Paul with the thought that even the stone-deaf could hear his bellowing voice. Bono in turn dubbed David Evans "The Edge" because of his sharp features and razor mind.

By the turn of the twenty-first century, rock 'n' roll no longer divided the generations. Anyone under sixty had grown up with it as a taken-for-granted influence that grew in breadth and intensity with the invention of more and more ingenious ways of rendering the music and lyrics omnipresent. Bono has written almost all U2 lyrics, and under the influence of such rock poets as Bob Dylan, the band has never shied away from political, social, and religious themes—making painfully personal what remains universally true across all generations, cultures, and classes: the pain of struggling to maturity, the ambush of death, the wrenching fellow-feeling between the world's spoiled and spurned.

Bono recalled that he "was never tormented in the way those early rock and rollers were between gospel and the blues. I always saw them as parts of each other. I like the anger of the blues—I think being angry with God is at least a dialogue."

Music can also bridge the gaps that divide people. Bono explained what moves him to write: "Music may not change the world, but it can certainly change the temperature. You know, when you're seventeen, or even younger? I was fourteen when I listened to John Lennon. I really felt that the world was much more malleable, really, than anyone else was telling me. That you could give it a good kicking and that it might change shape, that things do not have to be the way they are."

The stunning success of the band didn't cure Bono of his need to make a difference in the world rather than rest on his laurels. In a 1986 interview with *Rolling Stone*, Bono explained that he was motivated to become involved by seeing one of the benefit shows staged by Monty Python's John Cleese for Amnesty International in 1979. "It became a part of me. It sowed a seed." In 2001, Bono arranged for U2 to videotape a special live performance for that year's Amnesty benefit. Then after the Live Aid concerts in 1985, Bono and his wife, Ali, traveled to Ethiopia to see the situation there firsthand. The couple worked at an orphanage for a month, writing songs and plays to teach children lessons about things like health and hygiene. "I saw stuff there that reorganized the way I saw the world. I didn't know quite what to do about it. You can throw pennies at the problem, but at a certain point, I felt God is not looking for alms, God is looking for action. You can't fix every problem, but the ones that you can, we have to."

In January 2002 in London, Bono, along with Bobby Shriver and activists from the Jubilee 2000 Drop-the-Debt campaign, founded DATA (Debt, AIDS, Trade in Africa) as a multinational, non-governmental organization. "Unpayable debt" is a term used to describe external debt when the interest on a nation's debt's exceeds the amount that the nation produces, thus preventing the debt's ever being repaid. DATA was created to obtain equality and justice for Africa through debt relief, adjusting crippling trade rules, eliminating the African AIDS epidemic, strengthening democracy with education, and fostering more accountability by both wealthy nations and African leaders. Start-up funds came from the Bill and Melinda Gates Foundation, financier George Soros, and technology entrepreneur Edward W. Scott. Bono has circled the globe to convince world leaders to increase multinational concern for AIDS.

By the mere fact they are human, people in debt-plagued countries have the right to go on living—and, *ipso facto*, the right to what life inescapably requires: food, clothing, shelter, and basic health care. But AIDS has become the leprosy of our time, accounting for many more lives than even the Holocaust: 150 thousand every month. Thirteen million African children have lost *both* parents to AIDS; in a single year, three million children die of it; in that same year, a half-million African babies are born infected but could be protected by pills worth only thirty cents a day, if they were available. In Zimbabwe, life expectancy has plunged from sixty to thirty-three years. As Bono says, "It is no longer a matter of charity; it's a matter of justice. There it was in Leviticus. 'If your brother becomes poor,' the Scriptures say, 'and cannot maintain himself . . . you shall maintain him. . . . You shall not lend him your money at interest, nor give him your food for profit.'"

He goes on: "The poor are where God lives. God is in the slums, in the cardboard boxes where the poor play house. God is in the silence of a mother who has infected her child with a virus that will end both their lives. God is in the cries heard under the rubble of war. God is in the debris of wasted opportunity and lives, and God is with us if we are with them."

Bono forthrightly admits that he is "that most suspect of characters; a rock star with a cause." On December 15, 2005, Paul Theroux published an op-ed in the *New York Times* called "The Rock Star's Burden," criticizing Bono, Brad Pitt, and Angelina Jolie as "mythomaniacs, people who wish to convince the world of their worth." Theroux, who lived in Africa as a Peace Corps volunteer and a university teacher, added that "the impression that Africa is fatally troubled and can be saved only by outside help—not to mention celebrities and charity concerts—is a destructive and misleading conceit."

Bono has also been criticized for never publicly stating how much of his own money he gives to any causes. Bono's empire encompasses real estate, private-equity investments, a hotel, a clothing line, and a chain of restaurants. Along with fellow band members, he owns a stake in fifteen companies and trusts, including concert-booking agencies, record-production firms, and trusts that are mostly registered in Ireland. He himself says, "It's actually, I think, more honest to say we're rock stars, we're livin' it large, we're havin' a great time and don't focus on charity too much—that's private; justice is public."

However, Bono could just as well stay in his penthouse focused on his investments. Also, there are two radically different but equally important ways to confront world suffering: either of the hands-on variety in field hospitals and city soup kitchens or by achieving the wealth and position to command the attention of government and business leaders who can change the policies that engender that anguish. Dom Helder da Camara said, "When I gave bread to the poor, they called me saint. When I asked *why* they were poor, they called me communist."

It's one thing to confer with popes, presidents, prime ministers, or even lawmakers about favoring the voiceless. It's quite another to sit for hour after hour with some undersecretary of something or academic economists or World Bank bureaucrats, as Bono does. That also takes a load of faith. "I never thought I would get this un-hip," he says.

What surprises an outsider, mystified by both the brute force and the intricacies of rock music and lyrics, is not only Bono's almost mystical ability to touch and move hearts and minds but his seemingly untiring insistence on downplaying his personal abilities and achievements. "Celebrity is ridiculous, as we all know. It's silly. It up-ends God's order of things. I mean, nurses, firemen . . . you know, the real heroes, are underpaid. They're actually saving lives, all of that. And then you have rock stars and film stars. It's kind of obscene. But celebrity is currency. And I want to spend mine well. And it doesn't really matter if it's my ego in the end. If children are being inoculated, if there's wells being dug because of the fuss we kick up, it doesn't really matter."

"No, you can't love too much. You can't out-give God." He pauses. "But you should try, I think. That's where I'd like to spend the rest of my life."

Points to Ponder

1. Have you ever been tempted to step in and do an act of kindness—sit at lunch with some "leper" or tell bullies to lay off tormenting someone, but you were held back by a real inner discomfort? "What will my friends think of me? That I'm some kind of do-gooder?" And yet, who would really value the opinions of those who thought less of you for being caring?

2. Which approach to the problem of human suffering appeals more to you personally: taking off a year or so after college to work hands-on in the Peace Corps or some other volunteer agency, or spending that time preparing yourself with academic and social credentials to confront those higher-ups who can effect wider change?

3. Is it possible that all that preparation could wither idealism? At least some young people, for instance, set off to be doctors for the world's outcasts or pro bono lawyers for the indigent but end up stuck in a quicksand of college loans and, understandably, lower their sights to assure themselves of a debt-free, comfortable life. After that, they might be able to return to their adolescent dreams. In today's moral atmosphere, is such high-mindedness doomed?

twelve

. . . .

Viktor Frankl
. . . .

Holocaust Survivor, Therapist

1905–1997

Perseverance:

Pronunciation: \pər-sə-vir-ən(t)s\
Function: *noun*
Date: 14th century
1 a: firmly fixed in place : immovable **b:** not subject to change
2: firm in belief, determination, or adherence : loyal

◇◇◇

Slowly, drop by drop, pain scalds the soul, as the gods inflict wisdom on us, all unwilling.

—Aeschylus

◇◇◇

Therefore, since we are surrounded by so great a cloud of witnesses, let us rid ourselves of every burden and sin that clings to us and persevere in running the race that lies before us.

—Hebrews 12:1

As a teenager in the Vienna of the 1920s, Viktor Frankl did brilliantly in his studies, including a course in Freudian psychology. At sixteen, he began to correspond with Sigmund Freud. The great master responded to every one of Viktor's letters. "I sent him material which I came across in my extensive inter-disciplinary readings which I assumed might be of interest to him," Viktor explained. To the boy's amazement, Freud personally forwarded Viktor's scientific paper to the editor of his *International Journal of Psychoanalysis*, and wrote to the boy, "I hope you don't object." Viktor said later, "Can you imagine? Would a sixteen-year-old boy mind if Sigmund Freud asked to have a paper he wrote published?" Three years later, he was walking through a Vienna park when he saw a man with an old hat, a torn coat, a silver-handled walking stick, and a face he recognized from photographs. "My name is Viktor Frankl. Have I the honor of meeting Sigmund Freud?" he asked, whereupon the gentleman said, "You mean the Viktor Frankl at Czernin Gasse No. 6, Door Number 25, Second District?"

In 1930, after receiving his medical degree from the University of Vienna, Dr. Viktor Frankl headed a network of low-cost counseling centers, and when Austria plunged into depression, he had the opportunity to study out-of-work men and women suffering from severe psychological as well as financial depression. Without jobs, their lives seemed useless, so he advised them to take up volunteer work and dwell less on their feelings of inadequacy, and in a remarkable number of cases, the therapy worked. Also during that time he directed treatment of more than three thousand suicidal women over a period of four years at the Am Steinhof Psychiatric Hospital. With these severely depressed people, he took the dramatic step of asking: "What's stopping you from committing suicide right now?" When the women began to tell him what held them back ("My child. My fear of God. My novel. My sister"), the doctor then had something positive to work with, to motivate them to choose life rather than escaping from it.

Sigmund Freud began to see that the two great schools of Viennese psychiatry had no ways to cope with such an ingrained sense of meaninglessness that so many people suffered from. The school of Freud rooted all neurotic behavior in unresolved sexual conflicts arising during infancy and childhood; the school of Alfred Adler held that personality disorders result from excessive attempts to overcome feelings of inferiority. But his studies convinced Viktor of a third cause: the feelings of meaninglessness he had seen in his patients and the belief that they were "going nowhere." Viktor theorized that the primary human motivation was not repressed sexuality or the drive for power, but the search for some kind of meaning to validate one's living. By 1937, he was writing in international psychiatric journals about what would later be known as "logotherapy," literally, "healing through meaning."

With the Nazi invasion of Austria in 1938, Viktor, like other Jewish professionals valuable to the state, was allowed to continue his work as chief of neurology at the Rothschild Hospital in Vienna, the only medical facility in Austria still employing Jews. Most of the patients there were also Jews. At Rothschild Hospital, with his Gentile mentor, Dr. Otto Poetzl, Viktor began sabotaging the Nazis' euthanasia program, which decreed that "all life unworthy of life" should be systematically eliminated. This included Jews and non-Jews alike who were mentally retarded, psychotic, victims of senile dementia, had suffered incurable strokes, or were born with cerebral palsy. The two doctors methodically falsified medical records of brain-damaged or schizophrenic patients, changing the diagnoses to temporary disorders such as feverish delirium. They saved hundreds of helpless people.

But Viktor Frankl was not safe forever. He and Tilly Grosser were among the last Jewish couples allowed by the Nazis to wed in December 1941. By the next summer he and his wife and their extended family were rounded up and herded to the railroad station. At first, they went to Theresienstadt, a "model camp" set up by the Shutzstaffel (S.S.) military guard to deceive Red Cross inspectors about the nature of Nazi camps. Then, when the Nazi inhumanity could no longer delude even the most naïve, they were shipped off to Auschwitz, the Polish death camp. Viktor later remembered:

> There were eighty people in each car. All had to lie on top of their luggage. The carriages were so full that only the top parts of the windows were free to let in the gray of dawn. . . . The outlines of an immense camp became visible: long stretches of several rows of barbed wire fences; watch towers; search lights; and long columns of ragged human figures, gray in the grayness of dawn, trekking along the straight desolate roads, to what destination we did not know.

They would soon discover. As they got off the train and lined up, they moved slowly forward toward "a tall man who looked slim and fit in his spotless uniform." He eyed each newcomer idly, then pointed his right forefinger limply either to the right or the left. They had no idea that a finger pointing to the right meant work, a finger pointing to the left meant imminent death in the gas chambers. Viktor was pointed to the right. He had no idea both his parents had been pointed to the left.

Viktor was stripped, his entire body shaved, whipped through showers, and presented to young troopers who assigned him two yellow triangles—the symbol for Jews—to be sewn on his jacket and trousers, and a number. Viktor

Frankl was #119-104—the number tattooed on his forearm until his death.

The men slept in tiered bunks, each tier seven feet square, accommodating nine men sleeping directly on the boards. The nine shared two blankets, all forced to lie on their sides like spoons in a drawer, unable to turn over, sharing their lice but also the heat of their bodies. One night Viktor was tempted to wake up a bedmate suffering from an agonizing dream but stopped, realizing no nightmare could be worse than being awake in such a hell.

Six million Jews died in Hitler's camps. Few know that eleven million Slavs died as well, and for the same reason: Hitler believed them all to be *Untermenschen*, "less than human." Unlike the general impression, most of the victims did not die in the gas ovens but rather of starvation, overwork, fatigue, and typhus. The captives worked twelve-hour days on ten ounces of bread and a pint of watery soup. If there was a single prisoner missing at the morning or evening roll call (even if he were dead in a latrine), the whole camp had to stay swaying at attention, no matter the weather, until he was found.

Viktor said:

> Like nearly all the camp inmates I was suffering from edema. My legs were so swollen and the skin on them so tightly stretched that I could scarcely bend my knees. I had to leave my shoes unlaced in order to make them fit my swollen feet. There would not have been space for socks even if I had any. So my partly bare feet were always wet and my shoes always full of snow. This, of course, caused frostbite and chilblains. Every single step became real torture.

The prisoners' first response, of course, was utter shock at such pervasive inhumanity. But then, almost inevitably, to preserve sanity they fell into spiritlessness, some even into absolute absent-presence, a depression so deep the sufferers could not move, or wash, or leave the barracks to join a forced march. No appeals, no blows, no threats would have any effect. Those who reached that condition were sent quickly to the gas chambers. Viktor was convinced such men had lost all faith in the future, and he resolved he would find his own purpose in the midst of madness by preventing such total surrender, which led many to suicide by throwing themselves on the electrified wires or drinking the Lysol water used to treat those dying of typhus.

He urged his fellow prisoners to joke and sing, to take mental photographs of sunsets, to replay valued thoughts and memories. While digging ditches or laying railroad track, he himself spent hours having conversations in his mind with his wife, Tilly, unsure if she were even still alive. He found a most profound truth—and the foundation of his psychiatric belief—in the words of Friedrich Nietzsche: "He who has a *why* to live for can bear with almost any *how*."

Whenever there was danger of despair, Viktor insisted to himself and the other prisoners that they find an *aim* for their lives, a purpose, a meaning. "Think about those you love, one at a time, linger over their faces. Think of what you will do outside. If you believe in God, anchor yourself in him," he told them. No matter how their keepers could degrade their bodies, they could never destroy their innermost selves without the prisoners' cooperation. To submit internally to those in power was to cooperate in the rape of their own inner selves and the last vestige of their freedom. There was always that *ultimate* freedom: "to choose one's *attitude* in any given set of circumstances, to choose one's own way."

Viktor also taught that "being human always points, and is directed, to something or someone *other* than oneself—be it a purpose to fulfill or another being to encounter. A person can find meaning through work or deed, through the experience of real love or of goodness, beauty, art, or through his or her *attitude* when faced with tragedy."

After three years in captivity, during which time Viktor Frankl was shunted from the camp at Auschwitz to Dachau to Buchenwald, the war began slowly to grind down. The Russians had broken into Berlin, and the Allies were forging forward in the West. Most of the authorities and S.S. troopers had deserted the camp, and just as Viktor and a friend were about to slip through the open camp gate, a car moved forward into the opening, painted with a large Red Cross. It was over.

Then began a part of his life no less difficult than the camp: Schooling himself to live like a civilized human being again after three years surrounded by un-men. At first, the world was as shocking by contrast as the first weeks in the camp had been. Viktor found he had lost his mother, father, and brother. His wife had survived the camps, but tragically, had died within days after the liberation. Only gradually was he able to began to build a new life from the rubble.

From 1947 until his death at age ninety-two in 1997, Viktor Frankl served as professor of neurology and psychiatry at the University of Vienna. He was guest lecturer at Harvard, Stanford, Duquesne, and Southern Methodist and accepted twenty-nine honorary degrees. He wrote more than thirty books, most eminently *Man's Search for Meaning* in 1946, which he said he dictated in only nine days, having lived it every day for three years. The first segment of the book describes his experience in the camps, the second segment a brief explanation of logotherapy, and the third, "The Case for Tragic Optimism," makes clear how one's attitude can transform any suffering into life. The book has sold over nine million copies in twenty-four languages. In a 1991 survey of lifetime readers conducted by the Library of Congress, Viktor's memoir was chosen as one of the ten most influential books in America.

His own terse words sum up his philosophy—and his life: "To give light, you must burn."

Points to Ponder

1. "He who has a *why* to live for can bear with almost any *how*." When you've had a more-than-usual string of grim, unsatisfying days, what inner convictions keep you going? When your week's work seems to have very few (if any) tangible rewards, who are the people who give you a reason to keep going so that they can at least be proud of your persistence?

2. Here's a stickler: We all think we know, but what is the *meaning* of "meaning"? It has a serious connection to "purpose" and "significance." Think of a Salvador Dali painting where odd objects, out of proportion, hang limply in an endless landscape with no real landmarks. Think of a child, waking in the dark from a nightmare. She's lost and terrified. But she cries out and, in an instant, her mother flicks on the light, holds her and rocks her, and says, "Everything's okay, honey." At that moment, the child has meaning again. All of us need that reassurance, when life seems no longer to make sense: a conviction of "Mom." That's what "a philosophy of life" is: a background of tested landmarks. How do you begin to sketch such a philosophy of life for yourself?

3. Since your days in diapers, all kinds of voices (contradicting one another) have been feeding you propaganda to convince you what life is for, what will make you happy. Every ten minutes, for instance, commercials convince you that greed is a virtue, that "the more things you have, the happier you'll be." Many films, music, and other media give the idea

that self-indulgence is the ideal. Experience of church-going (as distinguished from heartfelt religion) can suggest happiness comes from avoiding sin and being other-worldly. Experience of schooling (again, distinguished from genuine education) can at least make mediocrity desirable: a D average gets the same diploma as an A+. Peers and parents (often at odds with one another) seem to say success comes from conformity. What truths does each propaganda system tell? What lies does it tell?

thirteen

●●●●●●●●●

Jackie Robinson

●●●●●●●●●●●●●●●●●●

Baseball Player

1919–1972

Dignity:

Pronunciation: \dig-nə-tē\
Function: *noun*
Etymology: Middle English *dignete*, from Anglo-French *digneté*, from Latin *dignitat-*, *dignitas*, from *dignus*
Date: 13th century
1: the quality or state of being worthy, honored, or esteemed
2 a: high rank, office, or position **b:** a legal title of nobility or honor
3 *archaic*: dignitary
4: formal reserve or seriousness of manner, appearance, or language

◇◇◇

*Joy, rather than happiness, is the goal of life, for joy
is the emotion which accompanies our fulfilling our
natures as human beings. It is based on the experience
of one's identity as a being of worth and dignity.*

—Rollo May

◇◇◇

*And when he was accused by the chief priest and elders, he made
no answer. Then Pilate said to him, "Do you not hear how many
things they are testifying against you?" But he did not answer
him one word, so that the governor was greatly amazed.*

—Matthew 27:12–14

Before Malcolm X and Medgar Evars and A. Philip
Randolph. Before Rosa Parks, and even before Dr.
Martin Luther King, Jr., there was Jackie Robinson.
He gritted his strong, white teeth long before other modern
greats struggled for more than token freedom for African
Americans. Before any civil rights lawyer or activist or
politician even came into the park, Jackie Robinson took a
heroic swing against indignity.

Jack Roosevelt Robinson was born in 1919, the last
child of five of a family of sharecroppers who eked out a
living on a plantation near Cairo, Georgia. Immediately
after Jackie's birth, his father deserted his wife and children. Jackie's mother, Mallie, felt the family might have
a better life if she moved them to Pasadena, California.
The move was not without cost. Mallie bought a house
in a mostly white neighborhood, and more than a few of
her neighbors begged the welfare agency to move them

somewhere else. "I remember," Jackie said, "even as a small boy, having a lot of pride in my mother. I thought she must have had some kind of magic to do all the things she did, to work so hard, and never complain, and to make us all feel happy."

While their mother did housework to support them, her children went to school and played sports. Jackie's brother, Mack, became a world-class sprinter, finishing second in the 1936 Berlin Olympics only to the great Jesse Owens. The one-two finish by the African Americans was an affront to Adolf Hitler and his notion of white supremacy. Jackie, meanwhile, was getting into trouble back at home. He filched groceries. He swiped golf balls from posh courses and then sold them back to those who had lost them. Luckily, he met a mechanic named Carl Anderson, who convinced Jackie that if he ran with losers, he'd *be* a loser. Jackie excelled at John Muir Technical High School, where he won varsity letters in football, basketball, baseball, and track.

His performance triggered college scholarship offers, and he accepted one to UCLA, where again he was a four-sport letterman. He stood out in football and was chosen to the All-American team as a halfback. During his senior year at UCLA Jackie met Rachel Isum, a freshman, the woman whom he would marry. Just months before Jackie was to graduate, he suddenly dropped out. He later explained that he was convinced that "no amount of education would help a black man get a job. It seemed necessary for me to relieve some of my mother's financial burden." World War II was approaching anyway, and the army drafted Jackie. After basic training, he applied for Officers' Training School. Even though he had nearly completed college, he was at first rejected until Joe Louis, the heavyweight champ, who was also at Fort Riley, stood up for him. In 1943, Jackie Robinson became a first lieutenant.

Even so, Jackie was only allowed to play baseball for the "colored" team at Fort Riley, not the main base team.

One evening in July 1944, Jackie was returning in a bus to Fort Hood, Texas, chatting with a fellow officer's wife, who happened to be white. The driver stopped the bus and told him he had to sit in the back with the other blacks. Jackie refused, knowing that recent publicity about black fighters Louis and Ray Robinson refusing to sit in the back of military buses had made the army forbid discrimination on its vehicles. Nonetheless, he was called up for a court martial, and though he was exonerated, he was tagged a troublemaker and removed from consideration for fighting overseas. Six months later, he received an honorable discharge.

From the army, Jackie went to play with the Kansas City Monarchs baseball team in one of the Negro Leagues that played apart from the all-white Major League baseball. Today, it seems ludicrous that a country which had just made untold sacrifices fighting a war to confront inhuman racial policies in Europe could still have "colored only" rest rooms, waiting rooms, even drinking fountains back home, as if skin color were somehow contagious. One New York councilman was so incensed by the inequity that he published a poster with two photos—one of a dead black soldier, the other of a black baseball player—along with the caption: "Good enough to die for his country but not to play baseball." The Negro Leagues were a bleak existence in many ways. Since most hotels and restaurants refused black patrons, players in the Negro Leagues often had to eat and sleep on the team bus. On the other hand, the money was good, and Jackie thought it was the only way he could, as a young black man, help his mother and make enough money to marry Rachel. He didn't realize fate was about to intervene. After only a year with the Monarchs, an Obi-wan Kenobi appeared in Jackie's life.

The new mentor was a white man named Branch Rickey, the owner of the all-white Brooklyn Dodgers.

When Rickey was a young coach at Ohio Wesleyan in 1904, a black first baseman named Charlie Thomas was one of his best players. When a hotel in South Bend, Indiana, refused Charlie a room, Rickey insisted the manager put a cot in his own room, as hotels then did for black servants of wealthy whites. That night, Charlie sat on his cot, weeping, rubbing his hands fiercely. "Black skin!" the boy sobbed. "Black skin! If only I could make them white." Rickey said later, "I vowed that I would always do whatever I could to see that other Americans didn't have to face the bitter humiliation that was heaped on Charles Thomas." He kept his word.

When Branch Rickey became president of the Brooklyn Dodgers in 1943, he had already created the farm team system in which major-league teams controlled minor-league franchises. The rosters of the many teams were peppered with players from all over the United States. Rickey also made it known that he was thinking about forming a Negro League, with a team playing in Brooklyn called the Brown Dodgers. Using the farm-team concept as a camouflage, Rickey sent scouts around the country to round up black talent for the Brown Dodger team that would never even be formed. His real plan was to open up all-white major-league baseball to black athletes and break the unspoken "gentleman's agreement" among white owners that had been in place since the nineteenth century prohibiting black players. Rickey figured that the player he looked for to shatter the barrier had to have more than athletic ability. He would have to have the inner courage and unshakable self-esteem to withstand all kinds of degrading abuse. The man he chose was twenty-six-year-old Jackie Robinson.

When Rickey met him, Jackie asked, "Mr. Rickey, do you want a ballplayer who's not afraid to fight back?"

and Branch Rickey answered, "I want a player with guts enough *not* to fight back."

Jackie began with the Montreal Royals, a Dodger farm team in the International League, and things did not go well. During spring training in Florida, Jackie was not allowed to room with the white players or even play in many ballparks. He did open the 1946 season as the Royals' starting second basemen in a game played at Jersey City. Many New Yorkers crossed the river to see not only one of the first ball games after the war, but the interesting sight of a black man integrating a white team.

Jackie's hands were sweating so badly he could hardly grip the bat and he grounded out weakly to shortstop his first time up. In the third inning, with two on and no outs, the Jersey Giants expected Robinson to bunt to move the runners along. Instead, he took a full swing and ripped the ball over the left-field fence for a three-run home run. In the fifth inning, Jackie bunted safely for a hit. Then he began to dance off the first-base bag in a way that would intimidate pitchers for years. He stole second. Then he broke for third. Then he stole home! In a 14-1 game, Jackie scored four runs, drove in three, and stole two bases.

But it was still going to be an uphill battle for Jackie. In Baltimore, fans screamed racial epithets at him for a full nine innings; in Indianapolis, the law prohibited him from playing; in Syracuse, an opposing player threw a black cat on the field, hollering, "Here's your cousin!" The International League's Little World Series was held in Louisville, a town that limited the number of black fans at its games. "I had been booed pretty soundly before, but nothing like this. A torrent of mass hatred burst from the stands with virtually every move I made," Jackie said. But he toughed it out, even if the Royals won only one of the three games. But in Montreal, home fans poured out to support a man they'd taken to their hearts. The Royals eventually won three more games and the Little World Series. At the end of the final game, they carried Jackie around the field on their shoulders. "Probably the only day in history," a sportswriter wrote, "that a black man ran from a white mob with love instead of lynching on its mind." One of the coaches, a Mississippian, told him, "You're a great ballplayer and a fine gentleman."

In 1947, Branch Rickey shrewdly decided to have spring training for the Dodgers and Royals together, and in Cuba, where there was no racial segregation. He told Jackie to impress the daylights out of the Dodger players and sportswriters, and he played sensationally. But it wasn't enough. The Dodger players still resented him. Some of the players started a petition to have him removed from the team. Rickey was determined, though, that his plan would not be stopped. He wanted Jackie to suit up with the Brooklyn Dodgers, and that is exactly what happened. He played his first game on April 15, 1947. Later in the month the team traveled to Philadelphia to play the Phillies. A chorus of venomous racial abuse poured out of the Phillies dugout, led by their manager, Ben Chapman. Jackie just kept taking deep breaths and clenching his jaw. He was, as one writer said, the only gentleman on the field. And it turned the tide. His Dodger teammates rallied to him. When bigots sent letters threatening Jackie's life, the team suggested they all wear his number so no one could tell which one was the black! After the season, *The Sporting News* named Jackie Robinson the first-ever Rookie of the Year.

Jackie Robinson played ten seasons for the Dodgers. In 1949, he had a .342 batting average, stole 37 bases, and was named National League Most Valuable Player. During his career the Dodgers played in five World Series, losing the first four to the New York Yankees while bringing cries from their fans of "Wait'll next year!" But finally, in 1955, with Jackie slowing up at age thirty-five and rumored to be retiring, the Dodgers beat the Yankees in seven games to win Brooklyn's first and only World Series.

In 1957, Walter O'Malley, the Dodgers' new owner, wanted to trade the aging Jackie Robinson to the team's bitter rival, the New York Giants. The Giants offered Robinson a contract for $60,000—a huge sum in days when a three-bedroom house sold for under $20,000. But Jackie said, typically, "It would be unfair to the Giants and their fans to take their money. The Giants are a team that need youth and rebuilding. The team doesn't need me." So he retired to become an executive with a coffee company. An eloquent speaker, he also served as an effective fund-raiser for the National Association for the Advancement of Colored People (NAACP). In 1964, he raised more than $1.5 million to found the black-owned Freedom National Bank to finance black businesses in Harlem. And in 1962, Jackie Robinson became the first African-American ballplayer to enter the Baseball Hall of Fame.

Jackie Robinson often told young audiences, "A life is not important except in the impact it has on others." And throughout his life he believed "the most luxurious possession, the richest treasure anybody has, is his dignity."

Points to Ponder

1. Few realize it, but we pay a heavy price for careless translations. Too often, translators render the Greek word *hubris* as "pride," as in "Pride always leads to a fall." Seems trivial enough, but as a result thousands of good-souled people grimly refuse to take rightful pride in any job well done. That is tragic because a Greek didn't mean by *hubris* honest self-esteem but "self-absorption, vanity, narcissism," the kind of arrogance that brought down the Caesars, Napoleon, and Hitler. Would those with well-grounded self-esteem ever degrade themselves to cheat on a quiz that in a week they'd

forget they even took? Consider: If you're honestly trying your best all the time, who could accuse you of vanity?

2. Humans are *invited* to rise above bruised feelings. When someone mocks you—with a racial slur or a snide remark about your taste in music or clothes or about your parentage or supposed sexual orientation—what factor within yourself would empower you to look at your assailant, shake your head, move on, and avoid a confrontation?

3. Branch Rickey, a white man, used all his considerable cunning to change an injustice that even many thoughtful African Americans were convinced was one of those "things that can't be changed." Why didn't he mind his own business and concentrate on winning games and keeping the status quo? Try to put into words what made him different from what you can gather about many sports owners (and movie moguls and real-estate tycoons) today. Then, being relentlessly honest, how was Branch Rickey different from you?

fourteen

· · · · · · · · · ·

Florence Nightingale

· ·

Nurse

1820–1910

Resolve:

Pronunciation: \ri-zälv\
Function: *noun*
Date: 1591
1: fixity of purpose : resoluteness
2: something that is resolved
3: a legal or official determination; *especially*: formal
resolution

◇◇◇

*You are a child of God! Your playing small doesn't serve
the world! There's nothing enlightened about shrinking so
that other people won't feel insecure around you! We were
born to make manifest the glory of God that is within us.
It is not just in some of us; it's in everyone! And as we let
our own light shine, we unconsciously give other people
permission to do the same. As we are liberated from our
own fear, our presence automatically liberates others.*

—Nelson Mandela

127

◇◇◇

*I urge you therefore, brothers, by the mercies of God, to offer
your bodies as a living sacrifice, holy and pleasing to God, your
spiritual worship.*

—Romans 12:1

The family house in Hampshire, England, had seventy servants. It was a world of whirl—operas, galas, grand balls, golf courses, riding to the hounds. Florence and her sister were formally presented to Queen Victoria when they were only in their mid-teens. Florence was very close to her father, who, without a son, treated her as his friend. He took personal charge of her education and taught her Greek, Latin, French, German, Italian, history, philosophy, and mathematics. She had offers of marriage from wealthy and titled suitors but rejected them all—to the utter dismay of her domineering mother. Then, in her early twenties, Florence had what she believed was an encounter with God. She became convinced she was called to make a difference in the world. However, she was mystified as to what specific way she would accomplish that.

When Florence turned twenty-five, she informed her parents of a decision that left them dumbfounded. Despite all her extraordinary advantages, she had the insane notion she would take up a lifetime of nursing. That was inconceivable, since in that age even the very remote smells of a hospital would make a well-bred young lady faint. Nevertheless, she insisted on visiting the poor and lower classes at local hospitals.

In a helpless attempt to deflect her foolish resolve, her parents sent Florence on a grand eighteen-month tour of the continent with family friends, Charles and Selina

Bracebridge. They traveled through Italy, Greece, and Egypt. On the journey from Paris, she met two St. Vincent de Paul nuns who gave her an introduction to their convent in Alexandria. There, Florence saw that the disciplined, well-organized sisters made better nurses than any she had ever seen. When the traveling party came to Germany—doubtless due to Florence's conniving—they spent time at Pastor Theodor Fliedner's unique hospital with a combined nursing school at Kaiserswerth near Dusseldorf. After she had returned to England, and undeterred by her parents pleas and threats, Florence returned for a full summer's studying at Kaiserswerth. Then she moved to a Sisters of Mercy–sponsored hospital in St. Germain, near Paris. On returning to London in 1853, Florence took up the unpaid position as the Superintendent at the Establishment for Ill Gentlewomen at No. 1 Harley Street.

In March 1853, when Russia invaded Turkey, Britain and France went to Turkey's aid in what became known as the Crimean War. But when British soldiers arrived in Turkey, more were dying from cholera and malaria than from battle wounds. Within a few weeks an estimated eight thousand soldiers were suffering from these two diseases. William Russell, the *London Times's* correspondent, described the terrible neglect of the wounded and pointed to the differences between the facilities provided for British and French soldiers. He asked, "Are there no devoted women among us, able and willing to go forth to minister to the sick and suffering soldiers of the East in the hospitals of Scutari? Must we fall so far below the French in self-sacrifice and devotedness?"

It was a moment for which Florence Nightingale's whole life had been preparing her. With a grant from the War Department and an assurance of full government backing, she left England with thirty-eight women, including eighteen Anglican and Roman Catholic nuns.

(It is worth noting that, for all her unarguable nobility, Florence was a flawed human being. She refused the service of Mary Seacole. Part of the reason was that Mary was Jamaican and seemed to some more priestess than nurse, though her later steadfast dedication in the same kind of Crimean hospitals—at her own expense—is evidence against that. Moreover, in proof Florence was no plaster saint, it was quite likely she refused Seacole's earnest offer of help because she was black.)

On November 4, 1854, Florence arrived at the barrack hospital in Scutari, a suburb on the Asian side of Constantinople. Her nurses found the conditions in the army hospital appalling. Men were kept in rooms without blankets or decent food. Unwashed, they were still wearing their battle uniforms. War wounds only accounted for one in six deaths. Typhus, cholera, and dysentery killed by far the majority. Florence later wrote:

> There were no vessels for water or utensils
> of any kind; no soap, towels, or clothes,
> no hospital clothes; the men lying in their
> uniforms, stiff with gore and covered with
> filth to a degree and of a kind no one could
> write about; their persons covered with
> vermin. We have not seen a drop of milk,
> and the bread is extremely sour. The butter
> is in a state of decomposition, and the meat
> is more like moist leather than food.

Men lay dying while rats sniffed around bits of rotting food, discarded by soldiers too weak to eat. A stench hung in the air from soiled sheets and from an overflowing cesspool next to the hospital.

From the outset, officers—and even military doctors—resented Florence's insistent views on hygiene. They were an assault on their own professionalism. And, after all, she was "only a woman" who seemed unnaturally opposed to accepting her God-given place in the order of things. Worse, she humiliated them with her reports to her contacts at the *London Times*. However, within ten days, fresh casualties arrived from the battle of Inkermann. There were over two thousand sick and wounded in the hospital, and in February 1855 the death rate rose to 42 percent. The War Office ordered the sanitary commissioners at Scutari to carry out Florence's reforms immediately. The doctors were so overwhelmed with wounded that they had no choice but to tolerate the intrusion of these knowledgeable, tireless women. Through the establishment of a fresh water supply as well as using her own funds to buy fruits, vegetables, and standard hospital equipment, three months later, the death rate had fallen to two percent.

Florence insisted she be the only woman in the wards after eight at night, when the other nurses' tasks were taken by male orderlies. She moved among the wards and got the name "The Lady with the Lamp" for her dimly lit walks. She secured the wounded men's pay and made sure it was sent home to their families, along with notes about their health. She established a library to nourish their minds as well as their bodies. She was one of the very few high-born ladies who could fathom their country accents.

On her return from the war, Florence had become a legend in her own lifetime. Honors came to her from every direction, but she pleaded with her influential friends to turn the attention from her onto the cause she represented. Her greatest achievement was to raise nursing up as a respectable profession for women. To spread her tested and proven convictions on reform, Florence published two books, *Notes on Hospitals* and *Notes on Nursing*, which were influential worldwide. Her concerns for sanitation, military health, and hospital planning established practices still in existence 150 years later.

In 1860, after receiving generous subscriptions to the Nightingale Fund, Florence established the Nightingale

Training School for nurses at St. Thomas' Hospital. The probationer nurses received a year's training, which included some lectures, but was mainly practical ward work under the supervision of the ward sister. Each day "Miss Nightingale" scrutinized the diaries and reports of probationary nurses.

In later life, Florence Nightingale suffered from poor health. In 1895, she went blind. Soon afterward, the loss of other faculties meant she herself had to receive full-time nursing. Although a complete invalid, she lived another fifteen years until her death in London on August 13, 1910.

A term that seems to fit Florence precisely is "resolve" (or perhaps more forthrightly, "stubbornness"). She refused to be diminished by the warped certitudes of her time. She protested the over-feminization of women into near helplessness, as she saw in her mother's and older sister's sluggish lifestyle, despite their education. She rejected their life of thoughtless comfort for the world of using her life to make a difference.

As one biographer wrote, Florence Nightingale's resolve "rode like a tank over machine-gun nests of red tape." She was a no-nonsense woman who steadfastly refused to be degraded. As she said, "No man, not even a doctor, ever gives any other definition of what a nurse should be than this—'devoted and obedient.' This definition would do just as well for a porter. It might even do for a horse. It would not do for a policeman." She confronted her society, and she refused to relent.

Points to Ponder

1. Our society has heroines and heroes who embody the glitzy ideals that the media so tirelessly offer all of us as the guarantees of "success": money, fame, sex, and power. But if their

success were genuine fulfillment, why do their lives seem to break down in drug use, failed relationships, and often even suicide? Do they finally kill themselves because they were so *happy*? Can anyone make sense of why they are even now still idolized? What modern insights to "happiness" was Florence Nightingale apparently missing?

2. Quite likely, given enough time, the enormity of human neglect in military—and civic—hospitals would have provoked "someone" to raise a ruckus about it and keep complaining until action was taken. But what had to have taken place *inside* people like Florence Nightingale to impel them to say, "Who, if not *me*? When, if not *now*?" To add to the inner problems anyone would face in such a cramped, seemingly powerless situation, she was a woman in an age when a respectable woman accepted that her role in life was to marry, run a household, and raise mannerly children. Has anybody ever told you to "mind your own business," "keep a low profile," or "don't make waves"? Are they right or wrong? At times, it is in fact genuinely futile to try to change a wicked situation, but less often than we might allow ourselves to believe.

3. It's clear that, though she turned out to be a heroine, Florence Nightingale didn't enjoy the approval or even grudging acceptance of many of the people she had to work with and for. "Will that confounded woman ever shut *up*?" you can almost hear them say. How much would the sneers and snarls of others discourage your willingness to stand up and be counted—even about something others think inconsiderable: the inflated cafeteria prices, doors off bathroom stalls for months, the habitually unprepared teacher, the constant bully?

fifteen

· · · · · · · ·

Tecumseh

· · · · · · · · · · · ·

Chieftain of the Shawnee Tribe

1768–1813

Honor:

Pronunciation: \ä-nər\
Function: *noun*
Etymology: Middle English, from Anglo-French *onur*,
honur, from Latin *honos, honor*
Date: 13th century
1 a: good name or public esteem: reputation **b:** a showing
of usually merited respect: recognition
2: privilege
3: a person of superior standing—now used especially as
a title for a holder of high office
4: one whose worth brings respect or fame: credit

◇◇◇

Rather fail with honor than succeed by fraud.
—Sophocles

◇◇◇

*"I command you: be firm and steadfast! Do not fear nor be dismayed,
for the LORD, your God, is with you wherever you go."*

—Joshua 1:9

There is a persistent, if baseless, arrogance in claiming Columbus (or Amerigo Vespucci, or the Vikings, or even Irish rovers!) "discovered" America. It's undeniable now that a great many nameless Siberians got to North America first. That vanity springs from the false conviction that no place on earth has a proper claim to existence until some European arrives there and "claims" it.

That same attitude gave false credibility to a belief called "Manifest Destiny," which justified any claim or action (even clearly inhuman) which furthered the occupation by European settlers of every acre of North America from the Atlantic to the Pacific. Proponents held that such a displacement was both unarguable (manifest) and inescapable (destiny). In his 1776 pamphlet *Common Sense,* Thomas Paine argued that the American Revolution was a providential call: "We have it in our power to begin the world over again. A situation, similar to the present, hath not happened since the days of Noah until now." In 1811, President John Quincy Adams wrote to his father, John Adams: "The whole continent of North America appears to be destined by Divine Providence to be peopled by one nation, speaking one language, professing one general system of religious and political principles, and accustomed to one general tenor of social usages and customs."

It's always shrewd to base one's claim to someone else's property on a promise from a God who can't be summoned to testify. This mindless argument rests on the same false assumption that one race and nationality of people is inferior to another. As history shows, since the beginning of humankind, some groups are always convinced that they have more right to this world's goods than anyone in their way. A median estimate from very sparse data suggests there were 50 million American natives in 1492. In the most recent census, 2.5 million Native Americans remain. No other ethnic group has suffered such diminishment.

One Shawnee warrior in what is now Ohio had the courage to stand and say to the approaching white settlers, "Thus far. No further!" His name was Tecumseh, or "Sky Panther."

In the wake of the American Revolution, arriving European refugees were cramped among diminishing resources to the East of the Appalachian mountains, eager to branch out into the wide-open country to the west—land that from time immemorial had known no owners, no fences, no deeds, where native tribes had without exception respected the land and its game. "Sell a country?" Tecumseh asked. "Why not sell the air, the great sea, as well as the earth? Didn't the Great Spirit make them all for the use of his children? The only way to stop this evil is for the red man to unite in claiming a common and equal right in the land, as it was first, and should be now, for it was never divided."

In September 1809, William Henry Harrison, at age twenty-seven the governor of the newly formed Indiana Territory (and later the ninth President of the United States), negotiated the Treaty of Fort Wayne in which a delegation of half-starved Indians surrendered three million acres of Native-American lands to the United States. This treaty was signed by Indians who didn't even live on the lands they ceded, and even though no Indian had the least notion of "deeds" or land-ownership.

Nearly a year later, on August 15, 1810, Tecumseh stood before Governor Harrison and told him:

> Brother, I was glad to hear what you told us. You said that if we could prove that the land was sold by people who had no right to sell it, you would restore it. I will prove that those who did sell did not own it. Did they have a deed? A title? NO!

He continued to list occasions when the whites had gone back on their word and finished with a chilling accusation:

> How can we have confidence in the white people? When Jesus Christ came upon the earth, you killed him, the son of your own God, you nailed him up! You thought he was dead, but you were mistaken. And only after you thought you killed him did you worship him, and start killing those who would not worship him. What kind of people is this for us to trust?

He assured the governor that Indian land was owned in common by all tribes together, from the Gulf to Canada, from the western prairies to the swamps of Florida, and thus no land could be sold without agreement by all. In the meantime, Tecumseh had united most of the tribes of the Northwest Territory and was on a mission to recruit all the tribes of the South. Governor Harrison was young, but also shrewd enough to take notice of this unique man. He wrote that Tecumseh was "one of those uncommon geniuses who spring up occasionally to produce revolutions and overturn the existing order of things."

Many warriors and their families from different tribal roots began to gather in a place called Prophetstown near the merging of the Wabash and Tippecanoe Rivers (near Lafayette, Indiana). The encampment was named after

Tecumseh's brother, Tenskwatawa, "The Prophet," who as a young man had been a roaring drunkard until one evening in 1805 when he drank himself into such a stupor his family gave him up for dead. The Prophet claimed, though, that he had journeyed to the home of the Creator Spirit, who told him to have the Indians give up all white customs and products, religious beliefs, farming practices, guns, iron cookware, and alcohol. Turning their backs on traditional ways had offended the Master of Life. If they returned to native customs, God would reward them by driving the whites from the land. Without his brother's charismatic vision and presence, Tecumseh could probably never have assembled six hundred mixed-tribe warriors and their families.

On November 6, 1811, while Tecumseh was in the South, Governor Harrison marched up the Wabash River with more than a thousand men to intimidate The Prophet and his followers. When the governor's forces approached the town, a young Indian rode out waving a white flag, with a message from the Prophet requesting a cease-fire until the next day, when the two sides could meet peacefully. Governor Harrison agreed, though he posted sentinels to guard his men on that cold, rainy night.

In the dark before dawn, The Prophet, convinced he was preempting an almost certain betrayal by the Americans, sent his warriors into the settlers' camp of mostly untrained volunteers. After two hours of back-and-forth combat, the Native Americans' ammunition ran low, and as the sun rose it was obvious how small The Prophet's army really was. The Indian forces finally retreated, herding their families out onto the plains beyond Prophetstown after pausing to retrieve their dead. Governor Harrison's men entered their deserted encampment and set the whole place ablaze, destroying not only their homes but their supplies for the coming winter.

In that one reckless act of attacking the Americans, Tecumseh's brother lost all credibility. When Tecumseh returned and faced The Prophet, he shouted in fury, "In one day! You have destroyed what I took ten summers to build and which now can never be rebuilt. In one day, you have destroyed the hopes of all Indians."

Still, the Indian alliance was battered but not broken. Now that the Americans were also at war with the British, "Tecumseh's War" became little more than a skirmish in what became the War of 1812, with Indians on both sides. Tecumseh joined the British side, and his men and battle skills were a major part in the American surrender of Detroit in August 1812. Before any battle could begin, Tecumseh marched his six hundred braves three times through a clearing in view of the fort to exaggerate their numbers, and the commander quickly surrendered to avoid a massacre.

This victory was short-lived however, because a year later American Commodore Oliver Hazard Perry won a sweeping naval victory on Lake Erie, cut British supply lines, and forced them to withdraw from Detroit. As they fled, the British burned all public buildings and retreated into Canada. Tecumseh followed, defending their rear against Harrison's 3,500 troops. Near Moraviantown on the Thames River in Ontario, the British commander decided to turn and make a stand in the open. The natives, however, were far more skilled at guerilla tactics and lay in ambush in a swamp. As Tecumseh predicted, the American cavalry were useless in the muck, and as they dismounted, Tecumseh's warriors leaped on them in hand-to-hand combat.

Unbeknownst to him, the British line had broken within the first five minutes, and the Redcoats were scattered through the forest, running for their lives. The full American force then swung round to the battle with the Indians in the swamp.

Gradually, the natives' war cries began to die as news spread among them that Tecumseh had been slain. The battle was over. So, too, was Tecumseh's dream of respect for his people and his hope for their rights in the Northwest Territory.

Nonetheless, he left a legacy of honor to shame his enemies:

> Show respect to all people and grovel to none. When you arise in the morning give thanks for the food and for the joy of living. If you see no reason for giving thanks, the fault lies only in yourself. Abuse no one and no thing, for abuse turns the wise ones to fools and robs the spirit of its vision. When it comes your time to die, be not like those whose hearts are filled with the fear of death, so that when their time comes they weep and pray for a little more time to live their lives over again in a different way. Sing your death song and die like a hero going home.

Points to Ponder

1. Whenever arguments over justice arise, almost always both parties agree that there exists a mutually accepted *norm* to determine acceptable behavior:
   - "Your foot was out of bounds."
   - "You landed on Park Place, so pay up."
   - "I worked all week for you; you owe me a salary."
   - "All human beings are created equal; they are endowed by their Creator with certain unalienable Rights, that among these are Life, Liberty and the pursuit of Happiness."

   How do you understand the principle of a "mutually accepted norm to determine acceptable behavior"? Do you accept the premise that such a principle can guide your personal behavior and the way you treat others?

2. As you read, was there anytime when you reacted negatively to Tecumseh and his people because they were fighting against *Americans*? If you've seen old black-and-white western films, you know many of them pictured those who opposed the whites as unbridled savages. The same was true in the earliest films of World War II when Americans encountered unscrupulous Japanese. During that war, many second- and third-generation Japanese Americans were rounded up and sent to concentration camps. However, German and Italian Americans were not, even though we were also at war with their native countries. How can anyone explain that?

3. Perhaps the most important question: Tecumseh spent a lifetime in an unsuccessful cause. Does that make him a loser? Who are other people who have had the similar experience of not reaching their life goals?

sixteen

· · · · · · · · ·

Nellie Bly

· · · · · · · · · · ·

Journalist

1864–1922

Spunk:

Pronunciation: \spəŋk\
Function: *noun*
Etymology: Scottish Gaelic *spong* sponge, tinder, spark
Date: 1582
1 a: vigor and strength of spirit or temperament **b:**
staying quality; stamina **c:** courageous readiness to fight
or continue against odds: dogged resolution

◇◇◇

We could never learn to be brave and patient
if there were only joy in the world.
—Helen Keller

◇◇◇

They replied, "Let us be up and building!" And they undertook
the good work with vigor.
—Nehemiah 2:17b, 18b

The word "shy" was never used to describe Elizabeth Cochrane. From her birth in western Pennsylvania during the last year of the Civil War, Elizabeth's mother dressed her in flaming pink clothing while other little girls were trussed up in sober brown and black or muted pastels. Her father, a wealthy judge, had ten children by his first wife, and after she died, he married again and had five more, the third of whom was Elizabeth, logically nicknamed "Pink," the most rebellious child in the family.

When she was only six years old, Elizabeth's father died. Unfortunately he did not leave a will, and in the legal battles that followed, her mother was left nearly penniless. Four years later, injudiciously, her mother remarried in the hope of providing for her still unmarried children, since it was unseemly that women of her station work. Her new husband was an abusive alcoholic, and Elizabeth's mother soon filed for divorce. Fourteen-year-old Elizabeth gave a devastating picture of her stepfather at the divorce proceedings.

Now left alone and without funding, Mrs. Cochrane had no choice but to work. She moved the family to Pittsburgh and opened a boarding house to support them. It was a tough town, and many old-timers of the late nineteenth century still objected to a woman taking work. One journalist in *The Atlantic Monthly* said Pittsburgh was like "looking into hell with the lid off." An op-ed piece in the *Pittsburgh Dispatch*, "What Girls Are Good For," scorned young women who were taking away men's jobs. The story served as a prophetic call to Elizabeth—an unwary commentary on the "subservient position" of women in society, while claiming that girls are useless outside of marriage. According to the story, any woman who tried to make a living outside that sphere, is nothing less than a monstrosity. Elizabeth shot off a fiery letter in reply signed

"Lonely Orphan Girl," and the editor was so struck by her passion (if not her unschooled spelling and grammar) that he asked the anonymous young woman to come forward and identify herself. When Elizabeth showed up, the publisher hired her as a reporter on the spot. But since her reputation would be compromised in a men-only profession, he gave her the misspelled penname from a song by Stephen Foster: "Nelly Bly, Nelly Bly, Bring the broom along. We'll sweep the kitchen clean, my dear, and have a little song!" For the next twelve years, Nellie Bly wielded that broom around the world with hard edged investigative reporting.

Nellie was one of the first investigative reporters. She often went undercover in various organizations and situations in order to write the stories from the inside. For example, she posed as an unwed mother to expose a baby-buying trade and as a thief to write about a night in jail. She also joined girls as young as nine or ten working in canneries, foundries, and glass factories. She could quote directly from factory girls who spent their idle evenings in pubs: "I have no money, I have no books, I have nowhere to go. I work all day in a miserable place. What do you want from me?" She posed as a poor sweatshop worker to expose the cruelty and dire conditions under which women toiled. She turned all her many amateurish short-comings into a sterling asset. With no formal education, no journalistic experience, no credentials whatever, Nellie became the eyes of her equally hampered readers and took them right into the scenes—with an uncanny sense for concrete details. She was no deep thinker; neither were her readers.

But when factory owners threatened to pull advertis-ing from the *Dispatch*, Nellie was forced to cover fashion, society, and gardening, the usual role for female journal-ists. But this feisty girl would have none of that, so she took a six-month working vacation in Mexico, sending back stories exposing the ruthless dictator Porfirio Díaz. The Mexican authorities threatened her with arrest, and she had to flee the country.

After all that excitement, there was no way Nellie would go back to covering garden parties, so at age twenty-four, she set off for New York. Her savings were drained after four months. Desperate, she sweet-talked her way into the editorial office of none other than Joseph Pulitzer's *New York World*. Pulitzer had designed his paper for the immigrants pouring into New York, with sensational stories about riots, murders, and disasters. He also hoped to educate them with crusading editorials, assimilating them into the American enterprise. Nellie Bly fit on the *World's* staff like a hand into a surgeon's glove.

Nellie's first on-the-job test was to get herself committed to the Blackwell's Island Insane Asylum for Women, a place so repulsive that author Charles Dickens cut short his visit there. Nellie was to report firsthand any abuses taking place there. To prove to the authorities that she should be admitted, she spent a whole night practicing different faces in front of a mirror before checking herself into a blue-collar boarding house. She refused to go to bed, shrieking at the other boarders until they called the police. Sent to court, the reasonably well-dressed girl with no identification pretended she had amnesia. The kindly judge called in reporters from all the newspapers to see if a story about this girl would bring forward her family. Several doctors declared her "positively demented . . . a hopeless case." The papers called her the "pretty crazy girl . . . with the wild, hunted look in her eyes," and her desperate cry: "I can't remember. I can't remember."

The food at Blackwell was mainly watery oatmeal, rancid meat, and bread that was no more than unbaked dough. Women sat all day in unheated rooms on hard benches. Nurses were abusive, yelling at the patients to shut up, and beating them if they didn't. "My teeth chattered, and my limbs were goose-fleshed and blue with cold. Suddenly I got three buckets of water over my head—ice cold water, too. I think I experienced the sensation of a drowning person as they dragged me, gasping, shivering and quaking, from the tub. For once, I did look insane." She included in one article a description of the screams of a young woman as attendants doused and beat her. (By the next morning the woman was dead.) Bly concluded that some inmates weren't crazy at all, just immigrants unable to protest because they knew no English.

In 1873, Jules Verne published a novel, *Around the World in 80 Days*, in which a cultured gentleman named Phileas Fogg accepts a large wager that he could travel around the world in eighty days. In the fall of 1888, eager to increase circulation of the newspaper, at a *World* staff meeting someone suggested the paper send a man around the world in *fewer* than eighty days. Nellie, infuriated, threatened to do it in less time for another newspaper if they didn't give her the job instead. She was a woman difficult to deny.

Nellie made her way by ship, train, carriage, donkey, rickshaw, sampan and catamaran—sending back tele-graphed reports daily, racing the clock at every juncture. Seventy-two days, six hours, eleven minutes, and fourteen seconds after she'd sailed from Hoboken, on January 25, 1890, Nellie arrived back in New York. At age twenty-five, Nellie Bly was the most famous woman in the world.

From then on, Nellie could pretty much name her own assignments. In 1893, she interviewed one of the most con-troversial political figures in the country, anarchist Emma Goldman. In Chicago, she covered the Pullman railroad strike from the strikers' point of view—even as govern-ment troops fired on them. But as the old saying goes, "Imitation is the greatest form of flattery." In the hope of duplicating Pulitzer's success, "stunt girl reporters" sprang up all over the country. Plucky young women—but never with the same flair as Nellie—visited opium dens, joined workers who rolled tobacco for cigarettes, went begging on the streets in rags, and collapsed on the street to gain admittance to questionable hospitals. They covered the wars in Cuba and the Philippines, prizefights, murder trials. Nellie had lost her distinguishing trademark to a host of better-trained, but less-qualified imitators.

At age thirty, Nellie married a seventy-year-old industrialist named Robert Seaman, president of the Iron Clad Manufacturing Co. For a very short while, she lived the life of a wealthy New York matron of leisure, but hardly for long. Probably out of sheer gilded boredom, Nellie eventually returned to William Randolph Hearst's *New York Evening Journal,* covering World War I at the frontlines with her usually gritty style. In one report she described a dead soldier she saw:

> One motionless creature had his cap on his head. Great black circles were around his sunken eyes, his nose and his ears were black. Near him, completely covered by his coat was a form. Occasionally it shivered convulsively. That was all. Human creatures they were, lying there in a manner our health authorities would prohibit for hogs or the meanest beasts. I staggered out into the muddy road. I would rather look on guns and hear the cutting of the air by a shot that brought kinder death.

During Nellie's coverage of the war Hungarian police arrested her as a British spy, despite her credentials. Then a translator arrived. "I am Dr. Friedman," he announced. "You are English, they say."

"I am Nellie Bly of New York," she answered.

"My God! Nellie *Bly!*" he cried. "Every child seven years old in America knows Nellie Bly!"

Nellie died of pneumonia in 1922. She had little money left at the time of her death, since the business she inherited from her husband withered away in embezzlements and lawsuits. What little she had left she donated to the care of an orphanage. As her biographer said, "She wasn't modest about anything." And another wrote, "Always, the main character in any Nellie Bly story is Nellie Bly herself, and she was very much a character." To some, such self-confidence is insufferably arrogant. But without such dogged courage, we'd probably still be cowering securely inside the caves.

Throughout her life, Nellie Bly's byword seems to have been what she wrote in her articles about braving the asylum: "I said I could and I would. And I did."

Points to Ponder

1. In a herd of people content to be silent and secure as sheep, anyone with true confidence is going to be considered arrogant. And sometimes that judgment is justified. Consider people like Eleanor Roosevelt and Florence Nightingale, who never sought notoriety for themselves. Or think about Oprah Winfrey, Jim Henson, and Will Rogers, whose work *depended* in large part for its effectiveness on being known. What motives make the difference between legitimate self-promotion and grandstanding, playing solely for the applause or shock? What shows some "different" people to be hollow and others profound?

2. Living in a home—even a wealthy one with servants—with fourteen siblings will surely have an effect on any child. Then facing a drunken and abusive stepfather, and then the further reduction into poverty would also shape a personality. Some young people might come through it resolute and aggressive like Nellie Bly; others might withdraw in defense against the pain and shame, becoming reclusive and shy.

The point is that, although others have been responsible for the child intuitively (without blame) developing those habits of coping, in adolescence anyone can take control of those habits and change them. Aggressive or withdrawn personalities are not incurable. Shy people can become assertive; pushy people can become thoughtful. The very first step is to analyze in which direction one is most often headed: Am I basically a battler or a brooder? Try to suggest to someone closer to either extreme of that spectrum what ways they could compensate for their personality's drawbacks and challenge its assets. "She turned all her many amateurish shortcomings into a sterling asset."

3. Do an Internet search for the poem "Curiosity" by Alastair Reid. It begins "Curiosity may have killed the cat; more likely the cat was just unlucky, or else curious to see what death was like." The poet argues that cats (and curious people) are adventurous, while most dogs (at least old ones) prefer "well-smelt baskets, suitable wives, good lunches." The poem's point is that curiosity won't cause anyone to die, only lack of it will. Without the courage to take *reasonable* risks, life is nothing more than "ODTAA." (Google that one, too!) He concludes the poem with: "dead dogs are those who do not know that hell is where, to live, they have to go." You probably have a vague hunch what that means, but try to put it into other easier words so you *really know* what it means.

William O'Malley, S.J., is a legendary high school teacher who began his career as a Latin and English teacher at Brooklyn Prep in 1957. He has taught English and Theology at Fordham Prep in the Bronx since 1987 and in 1990 was awarded the F. Sadlier Dinger Award for outstanding contributions to religious education in America. A great advocate of creativity and the arts, O'Malley has produced several videos and written ninety-nine plays and musicals. He is the author of hundreds of articles, and several books, including *Choosing to Be Catholic.*

Adolescent Resources

A Teen's Game Plan for Life
Lou Holtz

Best-selling author Lou Holtz draws attention once again to his wit and wisdom in *A Teen's Game Plan for Life*, an inexpensive and teen-friendly book that parents, coaches, and anyone who works with youth can use to motivate and inspire teens. After over forty years of dedication to molding teenagers into adults as a legendary football coach, including a national championship as the coach of the Notre Dame Fighting Irish, Lou Holtz shares a commonsense message with teens that is easily understood as a game plan for life:

+ Choose your attitude
+ Make sacrifices
+ Get rid of excuses
+ Dream big dreams
+ Understand what you're trying to do

ISBN: 9781933495095 / 128 pages / $10.95

Ready for College
Everything You Need to Know
Michael Pennock

Covering everything from saying good-bye to Mom and Dad to getting along with a difficult roommate, Michael Pennock offers advice to help students transition from high school to college. *Ready for College* encourages college students to develop their faith while away from home.
ISBN: 9781893732926 / 160 pages / $11.95

ave maria press
Phone: 1-800-282-1865 / Fax: 1-800-282-5681
E-mail: reled@nd.edu / Web: www.avemariapress.com
A Ministry of the Indiana Province of Holy Cross

Promo Code: F0A01090000